Naples
Secrets
in the Sun

Naples Secrets in the Sun

AS UNCOVERED BY AN INQUISITIVE UBER DRIVER

Alan Bianco

Published by Meaning of Life Press, Inc.

For more information, visit www.NaplesSecretsintheSun.com

ISBN (paperback): 979-8-9873147-0-8
ISBN (ebook): 979-8-9873147-1-5

Editor: David Aretha
Book design: Christy Day, Constellation Book Services
Cover photo and author photo: Sea Terri Photography and Terri Leach

City of Naples map used by permission of TDNaples.com Realty
Collier County map used with permission of Mapsofworld.com

Uber is a registered trademark of Uber Technologies, Inc.

Printed in the United States of America

DEDICATIONS

To my mother, Janet, who taught me how to drive.

And to Audrie Nubile, Geoff Chaucer, Miss Haertel[1], Aesop, Dr. Trinklein, William Gaines, Jean Shepherd, Bill Shakespeare, Abbie Hoffman, John of Patmos, Mario Puzo, Jerry Pournelle, Sam Clemens, Hunter S. Thompson, Dan Ingram, edward estlin cummings, and the late, great, P.J. O'Rourke, who showed me how to write.

And to the Naples Historical Society, who provided me with a lot of information on historical Naples, most of which I have twisted, bent, and distorted beyond all recognition.

And to Martha Bullen (World's greatest Publishing Consultant and Book/Life Coach), Christy Day (World's greatest Book Designer), Maggie McLaughlin (World's greatest Ebook Designer), and David Aretha (World's greatest Editor and Author Inspirer), without whose advice I would still be sitting in a corner, all by myself, trying to conjugate a verb.

Oh yes, I almost forgot. Thank you, God!

---

1   My tenth-grade English teacher who always told us never to begin a book with "Once upon a time. . ." and never to end one with ". . . and I lived happily ever after". Sorry, Elaine, my bad!

Contents

Introduction   1

Conventions Used in This Book   5

Chapter 1: Naples—The Backstory   7

Chapter 2: Uber and Me—The Backstory   31

Chapter 3: Lore, Legends, and a   41
Few Fun Facts Vis-à-vis Naples

Chapter 4: Reality, Truths, and a Few   71
Not-so-Fun Facts Vis-à-vis Naples

Chapter 5: Passengers—The Good, the Bad,   78
and the Ugly!

Chapter 6: A Death in the Family   127

Chapter 7: All Good Things . . .   129

Chapter 8: Denouement   132

The Naples Almanac   136

Introduction

ONCE UPON A TIME, I was a recently retired lawyer and a not-so-recently retired (but somewhat conservative) hippie, living in Naples Florida, an ageing (but lively), wealthy (yet diverse), and modern (yet historical) community, providentially located in the southwest corner of Collier County, which is in the southwest corner of Florida, which is in the southeast corner of the United States.

After a few years of retirement, I was beginning to get restless when, out of the blue (more likely out of China), our entire planet was enveloped by Covid. The onset of this virus intensified my restlessness, as did the requests, then demands, then orders from almost every political leader in America that we all "shelter in place," mask up, and lock down or the world would come to an end (or something like that).

As my restlessness increased, my long-lost, youthful, Hippie instinct to societally rebel suddenly and inexplicably returned! I guess Ponce de León was right; the Fountain of Youth *is* in Florida!

To combat my restlessness, I decided I had to do something. But what? I didn't know how to deal drugs, I was too old to become a gigolo, and I wasn't going to sit through another Bar exam. What, I wondered, could I master that didn't involve heavy labor, would be fun to do, would allow me to escape sheltering in place, and would let me enjoy all the wonderful Florida sunshine? (After all, my mother always told me to play outside when the weather was nice.)

After some intensive and extensive soul searching, I found my solution. To keep active, stay unsheltered, have some fun, and "fight the man" one last time, I decided to become an Uber® driver.

I took to my new vocation (and consequent passenger interaction) like a snook to a shallow saltwater flat[1] and quickly found myself driving at least eight hours a day, seven days a week. Almost as quickly, I discovered Marcie Blane[2] was right; I wasn't a kid anymore! I was having fun but I was wearing myself out. So, I had to force myself to take at least one day off each week, not to begin work until 7 a.m., and to come home at a reasonable hour every night (another of my mother's frequent requests).

Besides being a hippie, I also considered myself a cowboy at heart (partially because Wyatt Earp and I share the same birthday). Consequently, when I started driving, I imagined I was Randolph Scott, riding the trail alone, driving cattle (in my case, people) to the railhead in Abilene, Kansas (in my case, to locations in and around Naples), battling marauders and bandits (in my case, traffic and gasoline prices), collecting and dispensing dogies[3]…er, passengers…along the way. I even gave my mount[4] (an elderly, flame-red Audi) an authentic western name, Red Flame.

The passengers Red Flame and I encountered on our trail ride were a diverse lot. They came in all races, creeds (a fancy

---

1   A humorous Florida angling anology.
2   Marcie Blane's 1962 hit song, "Bobby's Girl," begins with the words, "You're not a kid anymore."
3   A cowboy phrase that means cattle.
4   A cowboy phrase that means horse.

legal word for religions), sexes, colors, ages, accents, body types, perfume/aftershave (and other) scents, personality types, political slants, hair amount and color, tat formats (the Blackwork School was the most common), and clothing (or lack thereof) styles. These eclectic passengers told me many eclectic tales. The most interesting ones were those of Naples, its history, and its people and those of life in general, its history, and its people.

Red Flame and I drove over four thousand passengers. And each one was unique, just like all the rest! They (and their yarns) were humorous, shocking, and compelling. So much so that I couldn't keep them to myself. I had to share them, but how and with whom? After much thought, I decided I would write a book to share my passengers, their tales, and a few of my driving escapades with the world's premier audience, you!

As I began to write, I discovered an inconvenient truth. I didn't know a damn thing about creative writing. I didn't know how or where to start, or what to say. I began to feel like an ignorant, out-of-focus, crazy man. I was really stuck.

Then, I remembered the words of Sherlock Holmes, who counseled. "Just observe what you see."

Sherlock was right. I took his advice to heart and discovered my reason, clarity, and sanity returning. I observed what I saw, listened to what I heard, understood what I researched, and then just wrote it all down. As the words began to flow, I found that writing was just as much fun as driving. So, I tried to write as hard as I drove (Editor's Note: He didn't drive that hard). The next thing I knew, the book was finished!

To make reading my work of art easy, I kept things simple. This book consists of only three main sections, three concluding chapters, and a helpful almanac.

The first main section provides a brief description and history of Naples and environs and a briefer description and history of Uber Technologies, Inc. (Chapters 1 and 2). Things lighten up in the second section where I share some fun (Chapter 3) and some not-so-fun (Chapter 4) facts about Naples and surrounding areas. The fun continues in the book's last main section where my most interesting passengers, their tales, and their antics are portrayed (Chapter 5). I found the passengers, their tales, *and* their antics captivating. I'm sure you will, too.

The final three chapters humorously wrap everything up.

Well, pardner, that's it. I'm certain you will enjoy reading this book. After all, I've used every literary trick in the book (so to speak) to hold your interest including, when necessary, good writing! If you enjoy this read as much as I enjoyed writing it, we'll both come out ahead!

P.S. Since I refer to many places in the book, I have added an almanac, containing maps of the City of Naples and Collier County, Florida, so you will understand where I am talking about!

"Things are only impossible until they're not!"
–J. L. Picard

Conventions Used in This Book

To illustrate, illuminate, and/or clarify both the stories in this book and life in general, as well as to generate a chuckle or two, I occasionally employ a few literary tricks of the trade known to more serious writers as conventions. They are:

NOTES ON THE MEANING OF LIFE

Scattered throughout the book are snippets of wisdom I call "Notes on the Meaning of Life." These snippets supply word definitions, famous quotes, Uber driver information, or general (but necessary) information on marine geology, history, geography, social science, Naples, films, and Earth science. Notes on the Meaning of Life will broaden your knowledge of both life in Naples and life in general. They will also eliminate your need to consult a reference book to understand what the heck I am talking about. Notes on the Meaning of Life are fun to read, personally empowering, and make great conversation starters at parties.

NAMES

Fictional Names—All passenger names in this book (except one) are fictional (but begin with the same letter as the individual's real name). This has been done to protect me from lawsuits, not to protect the innocent. They can fend for themselves.

TELLING THE TRUTH

Most of this book is true, but some is iffy. Areas of the book that stretch (or completely break) reality are (usually humorously) noted by the editor.

A NOTE ON PROFANITY

Since I am an OG, I am always opposed to profanity (unless I am using it). As such, I tried to write this book without any profanity. Unfortunately, I failed. While there is far too much profanity in today's works of "art," there is a definite (but limited) need for artists (like me) to employ profanity to express the lofty peak or abysmal nadir of human emotion or to make a definitive and/or humorous point. In a way, I apologize.

> **NOTES ON THE MEANING OF LIFE**—OG is slang for Old Guy!

SKEWERING

Throughout the book, I occasionally skewer people or ideas. Please be assured that it is always done in good fun and with good intentions. Usually.

CHAPTER 1

Naples—The Backstory

NAPLES VS. NAPLES VS. NAPLES

Before the secrets of Naples can be revealed, three geographic anomalies of the area must be explained. The first anomaly is that there is not one Naples, but three distinct areas that are commonly called Naples, Florida. The first is the City of Naples, a (very) irregularly shaped entity that hugs the Gulf Coast. It encompasses only 14.4 square miles, six zip codes, and, in 2018, it had a population of 19,539 (See Almanac A—Map of the City of Naples). In this book, this area will be called the City of Naples.

The second area commonly referred to as Naples is the populated area of Collier County (which includes the City of Naples). Most locals, as well as the U.S. Postal Service, call this region Naples. The populated area of Naples includes the Gulf Coast of Collier County from Marco Island north to the Collier County line and a large inland section north of Collier County's only Interstate, I-75. Although this area encompasses only about 250 square miles, when combined with Marco Island it holds over 90 percent of the population of Collier County. (The populated area of Collier County is shaded gray on the map in Almanac B—Map of Collier County and County Regions.) In this book, I will refer to this area as "the populated area of Naples" or just Naples.

The final area referred to as Naples is the metropolitan statistical area (MSA) of Naples/Marco Island.

NOTES ON THE MEANING OF LIFE—An MSA, formerly a Standard Metropolitan Statistical Area (SMSA), is a region consisting of a city and surrounding communities linked by social and economic factors as determined by the Office of Management and Budget.

The Naples/Marco Island MSA is all of Collier County, which includes the cities of Everglades City, Goodland (not actually a city, a CDP, which is government speak for *Census Designated Place*, really!), Immokalee (also a CDP), Marco Island, and Naples. Collier County encompasses 2,305 square miles, seventeen Zip codes and, in 2022 had a population of 405,005. In this book, I will refer to this area as Collier County.

DIRECTIONAL TERMINOLOGY

The second local anomaly is that there are two unincorporated communities in the populated area of Naples—North Naples and East Naples—that are now paradoxically misnamed. When these communities were founded, they were, respectively, on the northernmost and easternmost edges of the then populated area of Naples. However, thanks to Naples' never-ending population growth, this is no longer the case. North Naples is now in the west-central part and East Naples in the central part of the populated area of Naples.

Therefore, when I refer to North Naples, I mean the neighborhood of North Naples (which is now west-centrally located), and when I refer to East Naples, I mean the neighborhood of East Naples (now centrally located). When I am talking about other areas in the northern or eastern parts of the populated areas of Naples, I will call them the northern or eastern areas of Naples.

NORTH VS. SOUTH IN NAPLES (AVENUE-WISE)

Its streets are Naples' final geographic anomaly. Like New York City, the streets of Naples are laid out on a grid. Unlike New York City, however, Naples' streets run north–south and its avenues run east–west. Also, unlike New York City, the numbering of the avenues in downtown Naples doesn't start in the east and move west; it starts at Central Avenue (which is sort of, kind of, but not really, in the center of it all) and moves both north and south. Avenues north of Central Avenue have "North" appended to their name (i.e., Fourth Avenue North), while the avenues south of Central Avenue have "South" added to their name (i.e., First Avenue South). Newcomers to Naples (except those from New York City) often find the street numbering system confusing.[5]

A TALE OF TWO DOWNTOWNS

Unlike Gaul, downtown Naples is divided into only two parts.

---

5   Even more so because Collier County has several other pockets of streets and avenues whose enumeration also begins with 1. These pockets are designated by different geographical suffixes (e.g., Fifth Avenue SW). In many cases, however, these directional suffixes sometimes make no sense. For instance, Fifth Avenue SW is eleven miles northeast of downtown Naples' Fifth Avenue S.

The fancier, more expensive downtown is Fifth Avenue South from Tamiami Trail to Third Street, while the (very) slightly less fancy and (very) slightly less expensive downtown is Third Street, south of 11th Avenue South. Each of these areas caters to a different clientele. Fifth Avenue serves older northern transplants, while Third Avenue takes care of the nouveau riche post-adolescents (also usually from the north). Hence, the Third Street downtown, while being physically older than Fifth Avenue, sports a (very) slightly less aged population!

> **NOTES ON THE MEANING OF LIFE**—*Gallia est omnis divisa in partes tres* (Gaul is divided into three parts) is the first line of Julius Caesar's classic memoir, *Commentaries on the Gallic War*. In case you're interested, the parts were Celtica (the middle of modern France and Switzerland), Belgica (Belgium, Holland, and a chunk of northern France), and Aquitania (the southwest corner of modern France).

A WORD ON WEATHER

Naples has two seasons, summer and not summer. During summer (late May to mid-October), the daytime high temperature is always between 90^0 and 95^{06}, the nighttime low is always between 70^0 and 76^0, and it rains heavily for fifteen minutes every day at 3 p.m. During not summer, the daytime high is always between 65^0 and 80^0, the nighttime low can drop into the 30s (Brrr.), and rain is scarce.

---

6   It never gets much hotter. The highest temperature ever recorded in Naples was either 99^0 or 100^0, depending on the source of the information.

> **NOTES ON THE MEANING OF LIFE**—In recent history, snow visited Naples only once, brief flurries in 1973.

A BRIEF AND CANDID HISTORY OF NAPLES

Naples was founded as a Greek colony (first as Parthenope, later as Neapolis) in the second millennium BCE on the west coast of the Italian peninsula. (Editor's Note: Wrong Naples!)

(Author's Note: Got it!) Naples, Florida was originally the home of the Calusa (aka Caloosa) Indigiens (fka Indians). Check that, Naples was originally the home to no one, but the Calusas showed up somewhere between three thousand and five thousand years ago and hung around until the Spanish decimated and dispersed them in the 1500s.

The first non-indigenous settlement in Southwest Florida of any appreciable size was at Fort Myers. Fort Myers, now a city of 83,505 about twenty-five miles north of Naples, used to be a real fort that was first garrisoned in 1841. It was later abandoned after the Seminole wars in 1858 but reoccupied by the damn Yankees in 1863, who held the fort for the balance of the Civil War. This occupation is the first reported instance of unneeded and unwanted northern immigration into Southwest Florida.

> **NOTES ON THE MEANING OF LIFE**—Fort Myers was the site of the southernmost battle of the Civil War in 1863. (Author's Note: Fort Myers was named after Oscar Mayer, the inventor of the hot dog!) (Editor's Note: 1. Fort Myers was named after U.S. Colonel Abraham C. Myers; 2. Oscar Mayer did not invent the hot dog!)

Settlers first arrived in the Naples area shortly before the Civil War and began a farming community. The settlers became known as crackers. Why is not clear. One theory is that the name arose because the settlers ate cracked corn. Hmmm, it's a good thing they didn't eat the local shellfish or Naples would have been founded by crabs!

Nothing much else happened in as yet unnamed Naples until the early 1880s when Roger Gordon and Joe Wiggins came to "town." Gordon had a pass (Gordon Pass, which is near where he originally settled), a river (Gordon River), and a few roads named after him, while Wiggins lent his moniker to another pass (Wiggins Pass, which is near where he originally settled), a state park (Delnor Wiggins State Park), and a few different roads.

> **NOTES ON THE MEANING OF LIFE**—If you are not nautically inclined, a pass is an opening or channel through barrier islands that is used to gain access to a bay or river.

Gordon and Wiggins were followed in 1885 by Confederate General and US Senator from Kentucky John S. Williams and Walter N. Haldeman, publisher of the Louisville *Courier-General*. They led a group of families to what is now Naples Bay. (More unneeded and unwanted northern immigration!) Promoters described the local bay as "surpassing the bay in Naples, Italy" and the name stuck.

Williams and Haldeman eventually built a general store, a post office, and a six-hundred-foot T-shaped pier into the

Gulf of Mexico that became home to the steamship *Fearless*. The pier has been destroyed by storms and rebuilt three times (and severely damaged by Hurricane Ian in 2022).

NOTES ON THE MEANING OF LIFE—Lee County was named for one Confederate general (Robert E. Lee) and Naples was founded by another. What political incorrectness!

In the fall of 1886, the Naples Town Improvement Company was founded to establish a town named Naples and develop it as a winter retreat.[7] Things took a lot longer than expected and Naples wasn't finally established as a town until December 1923. The nascent town didn't hold its first Town Council meeting until April 13, 1925, sixteen months after its founding. Small government at its finest!

In 1911, the final major player and "almost a founder" of Naples, Barron Gift Collier (unfortunately, another northern interloper, worse, a New Yorker—Fortunately, he was born in Memphis, Tennessee) arrived. Collier was an advertising entrepreneur who became the largest landowner in Florida, eventually owning over one million acres. (Yeah, his family held onto some of it!) He also owned a chain of hotels, a few bus lines, several banks, a couple of newspapers, a telephone company, and a steamship line.

---

7   It took a while, but eventually the Improvement Company succeeded beyond their wildest expectations!

> **NOTES ON THE MEANING OF LIFE**—Collier, who was good friends with both J.P. Morgan and Franklin D. Roosevelt, had an interesting financial career. In 1915, he earned the highest income in the United States ($10 million) but went bankrupt in the 1930s.

Collier changed the face of Naples more than anyone else. In 1922, he financed the completion of the Tamiami Trail. (Which runs through the Everglades from Tampa to Miami; hence its name, a contraction of Tampa and Miami!)

> **NOTES ON THE MEANING OF LIFE**—As you can imagine, dredging and roadbuilding through the Everglades in the sweltering summer engendered many problems. The biggest of these was mosquitos. (The Everglades is, after all, the biggest sub-tropical swamp in America.) Baron Collier's employees used alcohol to mask the mosquito problem. But they didn't apply it, they drank it! Several passengers, who were descendants of men who worked on the project, told me that most of the dredgers and road builders drank copious amounts of alcohol every day to ease the mosquito problem, or at least make it ignorable. These passengers also said that the dredging company supplied the alcohol!

When the Tamiami Trail's roadbed was laid through the Everglades, it created an impermeable barrier. This barrier caused all saltwater plant and animal life north of the trail and all freshwater plant and animal life south of the trail to die ignominious deaths. No one noticed (nor did the world come to an end), until recently. In 2017, the State of Florida began replacing 10.7 miles of the Tamiami Trail roadbed with water-permeable bridges so the father of swamps can again go unvexed to the sea.

> **NOTES ON THE MEANING OF LIFE**—In July 1863, after General Grant captured Vicksburg, Mississippi, giving the Union control of the entire Mississippi River, Abraham Lincoln remarked, "The Father of Waters again goes unvexed to the sea."

Collier went on to invest millions of dollars in Naples and environs.[8] As a show of appreciation, almost everything in the county was named after him, including the county itself (Collier and Hendry counties were created from parts of Lee County in 1923[9]). The Collier family is still active in Naples. In fact, Barron's grandson, Miles, founded the Revs Institute for Automotive Research in 2008. Revs is one of the finest automobile collections in the world and a great place to visit, even for those who aren't car enthusiasts. The institute is open to the public on Tuesdays, Thursdays, and Saturdays.

Slowly, Naples began to grow. Electric service arrived in 1926, and the first railroad train, the Orange Blossom

---

8   Among other things, Barron Collier pioneered the use of yellow and white dividing lines on roads.

9   Partially because Lee County couldn't pay its bill for the Tamiami Trail.

Special, steamed into Naples Depot in 1927. (Now the site of the charming—and free—Naples Depot Museum.)

NOTES ON THE MEANING OF LIFE—Speaking of electric service, there is an electrifying and moving museum in Fort Myers called the Edison Ford Winter Estates. As the name implies, the museum consists of the former winter homes (and laboratories) of Thomas Edison and Henry Ford, who electrified and moved the country (and fortuitously lived next to each other).

Naples includes many celebrities in its citizenry today (See Chapter 3 Napoletani Straordinario), but the first to "land" in the area were Charles and Anne Morrow Lindbergh, who vacationed on Sanibel Island in the 1930s. One day in 1932, when Lindbergh needed supplies, he flew to Naples and landed his plane on a golf course that was at Third Street and Fifth Avenue South.

During World War II, Naples did its part. Numerous airfields were built in the surrounding area by the Army Air Corps. At least three of which still operate today: Naples Airport, Punta Gorda Airport, and Immokalee Regional Airport.

Naples was incorporated as a city on May 25, 1949. But just as the population and popularity of Naples began to grow, disaster struck! On September 10, 1960, at high noon, Hurricane Donna made landfall right on top of Naples. Donna did deep damage; over 360 lives were lost and property damage approached $1 billion (in 1960 dollars!).

Although Naples was ravaged by Donna, Everglades City, thirty-six miles southeast of Naples, was utterly destroyed. Everglades City was the seat of Collier County, but due to the destruction wrought by Donna, Collier County moved the county seat from Everglades City to Naples (to be precise, to East Naples) in 1962.

> **NOTES ON THE MEANING OF LIFE**—Donna was a brutal storm. At its peak, the tidal surge at intersection of Fifth Avenue South and Tamiami (about a mile inland) exceeded three feet!

Despite Hurricane Donna, Naples kept growing. As shown on the following U.S. census chart, Collier County has grown rapidly since its inception in 1923. Since most of the area's growth occurred after 1960, Naples is a very "young" city (infrastructure age, not resident age). In fact, the average house in Naples was built in 1990.

Collier County Population		
Year	Pop.	%±
1930	2,883	—
1940	5,102	77.00%
1950	6,488	27.20%
1960	15,753	142.80%
1970	38,040	141.50%
1980	85,971	126.00%
1990	152,099	76.90%
2000	251,377	65.30%
2010	321,520	27.90%
2020	375,752	16.90%
U.S. Census		

A BRIEFER, BUT STILL CANDID HISTORY
OF PLACES NEAR NAPLES

Marco Island

Marco Island is a barrier island south of the City of Naples. (See Almanac B—Map.) The City of Marco Island occupies the entire island. Marco, as the natives call it, was originally incorporated as Collier City in 1927. Then, mainly because no one lived there, it was unincorporated in 1957. Finally, it was re-incorporated as the City of Marco Island on August 28, 1997. Today, Marco houses almost as many residents (17,692 in the summer, about 40,000 in the not summer) as the City of Naples (19,539 in the summer, about 48,000 in the not summer).

Marco Island was so named because it was discovered by Marco Polo in 1291. Marco (Polo, not Island) was trapped in China because the Silk Road had become flooded with refugees and was impassable. He decided to return to Venice by boat but ran into Central America (which wasn't on his charts because it hadn't been discovered yet!). He made his way through the Panama Canal (which was unmanned in those days) and continued sailing across the Caribbean Sea until he ran aground on Marco (the island, not Polo), just north of today's Tigertail Beach. Proof of Polo's discovery was recently confirmed when three packages of fossilized Ramen Chinese noodles (Lime Chili Shrimp Flavor) were discovered at an ancient Calusa Indian camp being excavated near the beach. The noodles were radiocarbon dated to August 23, 1291, and three sets of Polo's fingerprints were lifted from the plastic wrapper. (Editor's Note: This paragraph is not accepted by ~~most~~ any historians, who believe Marco Island got its name from Spanish explorers who called it La Isla de San Marcos after Gospel writer St. Mark.)

In 1871, W.T. Collier and his family (who were not related to the Barron Collier) arrived on the Island and started a small fishing and clamming business. In 1883, W.T.'s son, W.D. "Captain Bill" Collier, became the town's first postmaster. Captain Bill's relatives still live on Marco Island today!

Except for the arrival of W.T. and family, Marco remained relatively quiet until the 1960s, when the Mackle brothers—Elliott, Robert, and Frank Jr.—began developing the island. (Interestingly, they bought the island from, you guessed it, Barron Collier.) They drained the island's eastern and southeastern swamps and built roads, bridges, one hundred miles of canals, and their own private hotel.[10] Later, they sold building lots for $2,550 to $16,000 and completed homes for $14,900 to $41,500.

There are a few reminders of the Mackle brothers left on Marco. The most obvious, yet most secret, is that several roads on Marco bear the name Elkcam. The secret? Elkcam is Mackle spelled backwards.

There are three bridges of note on Marco. The main bridge entering the island[11] is named the Jolly Bridge because everyone feels jolly when they arrive on Marco. A second bridge, located halfway down Collier Avenue, the island's main street, is named the Savage Bridge because everyone

---

10 Originally called the Marco Beach Hotel and Villas. Now it is the JW Marriot Hotel.

11 There is also a second bridge entering the island at Goodland.

has a savage good time on Marco. Finally, the main bridge leaving Marco is called the Bridge of Sighs because everyone sighs sadly when they leave Marco. (Editor's Notes: 1. The bridge entering Marco is the S.S. Jolley Bridge. It was named for former Collier County Judge Seward S. Jolley. 2. The Savage Bridge was named in honor of Herbert R. Savage, Esq., who was the Mackles' lawyer. 3. The bridge leaving Marco Island is merely the second span of the S.S. Jolley Bridge. 4. The Bridge of Sighs is in Venice, Italy.)

> **NOTES ON THE MEANING OF LIFE**—There are many fine (and a few not-so-fine) restaurants on Marco. Unfortunately, they all tend to close early. In fact, 9 p.m. is known locally as "Marco Midnight."

After the Mackles had developed about half the island, the newly minted Environmental Protection Agency (EPA) halted further development, ostensibly to prevent environmental damage.

Today, Marco Island, just like Gaul, <u>is</u> divided into three parts. The eastern and southeastern parts of the island that were developed by the Mackles are now heavily populated, successful, and thriving (although environmentally damaged). The middle of the island, thanks to the EPA, is still the alligator-infested, marshy, mosquitoed[12], yet environmental undamaged swamp it always was. But there is light at the end of the island. On the eastern shore of Marco is a village

---

12   Mosquitoed is a word I had to invent this word to illustrate the fine work of the EPA. It is the adjective form of the noun *mosquito*.

called Goodland that was founded by Johnny Roberts (No relation to the Chief Justice of the United States) in the late 1800s. He named it Goodland because it contained a forty-acre shell mound left by the Calusa Indians that was ideal for growing fruit and vegetables and because Goodland sounded like a better name for a village than Goodshellpile. The name stuck and today Goodland is a honky-tonk hamlet of four bars, three marinas, a post office, and a Baptist church. Everyone has fun in Goodland.

Everglades City

Nowadays, Everglades City is only semi-aptly named. While it is located smack-dab in the Everglades, but it is not really a city, at least not anymore. Most of Everglades City was destroyed by Hurricane Donna in 1960. The damaged buildings were removed, but weren't replaced, leaving the bizarre sight of numerous large buildings, many of brick or stone, surrounded by acres of empty land. Today, Everglades City has a population of only 353.

Everglades City Hall Standing Alone

City Hall in Everglades City is an impressive, two-story, white stone building. It has a portico in the front and the roof is supported by classic Greek columns. Yet it sits all by itself, in the middle of nowhere! Likewise, the Everglades Bank Building sits where it always sat, but now it sits there alone. Everglades City looks like a giant had sprinkled several large buildings in the middle of a large open field. Walking/hiking through the area just to view the surviving buildings is worth the trip.

The Everglades Bank Building in Everglades City

Except for a few restaurants,[13] the only commercial industries remaining in Everglades City are airboat trips and drug smuggling. Airboat trips are open to the public and take tourists and Floridians alike on dazzling trips through the Mangrove swamps of the Everglades. The flora and fauna that can be seen on these trips are stunning!

---

13   If you enjoy classic architecture, visit the Everglades City Rod and Gun club. The food is average at best and the facility is a little run-down, but the solid wood dining rooms and hallways (and bar) are spectacular.

> **NOTES ON THE MEANING OF LIFE**—Anyone taking an Everglades airboat trip should be sure to board a boat that has passenger headphones. Airboat engines are loud, and if headphones aren't provided, the captain's commentary will be drowned out by the noise of the engine.

Drug smuggling is the other major industry in Everglades City. This industry, for the most part Everglades, is not open to the public. A small group of professionals (and a larger group of amateurs) smuggle just about anything (but mostly drugs) into Everglades City. Drug busts are common and it is not unusual for the quantity of drugs seized during these busts to be staggering (I said it was a major industry). In October 2019, 28,000 pounds of cocaine and 11,000 pounds of marijuana were seized by the Coast Guard and, incredibly, in the 1980s, 256 men—over 70% of the adult male population of Everglades City—were arrested for drug smuggling. The arrestees were charged with retrieving illicit drugs by collecting drug bales left in the swamp by foreign smugglers; a practice known locally as "fishing for square grouper[14]".

Early in my Uber career, I drove a Coast Guard investigator and asked him if these drug seizures were for real. He told me not only were they real, but they were only a small fraction of all the drugs seized. Most drug seizures, he said, were not publicized.

---

14 Apparently, the name "square grouper" arose because marijuana bales are somewhat square (In fact, they are rectangular. Apparently, drug dealers have as little regard for geometry as they have for the law!).

Everyone in Everglades City is aware of the local smuggling activity. Almost everyone also has a friend or family member who was arrested and subsequently, in local lingo, "went to college" (i.e., jail).

Keewaydin Island

Like Marco Island, Keewaydin Island is also a barrier island just off the Gulf Coast between the City of Naples and Marco Island (See Almanac A—Map). In the summer, Keewaydin is home to throngs (some wearing thongs) of boaters, who beach their boats and enjoy the sunshine. In the winter, a much smaller coterie (some wearing coats) of diehard boaters "hit the beach." When the beaches of Keewaydin are hopping, many commercial boats land there and sell their wares (food and ice cream, but not coffee) right off the boat. Liquor is also sporadically available on Keewaydin, but you have to find out where it is and through whom to obtain it.

Evidence has recently been uncovered suggesting Marco Polo was also responsible for giving Keewaydin Island its name. When Polo sailed past the island in 1291, a few Calusa Indians started walking into the surf toward his ship. Polo, excited at meeting them, told them to "keep wading." Unfortunately, because of his Venetian accent and the fact he mumbled a lot, the Indians heard his instruction as Keewaydin. (Editor's Note: Not even close. The island was originally called Kee Island. After it became part of the Keewaydin Camps Ltd. Corporation in the 1893, it became known as Keewaydin Island. Marco Polo had nothing to do with it, he was long dead by then.)

Golden Gate Estates

Golden Gate Estates (known locally as The Estates) is a huge (about ninety-one square miles) region to the east (and north and south) of the populated area of Naples. Large parts of The Estates were bought in the 1960s by Gulf American Corp., an assemblage of businessmen of questionable ethics who tried to sell building lots to the public. They dug canals for drainage, laid roads, pressured a local airline company to fly prospective buyers over the area, and used high-pressure sales tactics to sell five-acre lots to the public. Unfortunately, a lot of the land they sold was swampy, inaccessible, or otherwise encumbered, and Gulf American Corp. went bankrupt in 1974.

> **NOTES ON THE MEANING OF LIFE**—Thanks, in part, to the Gulf American Corp., any bad business deal today is analogized to "buying land in Florida."

The Estates remained quiet until recently when parts of it began growing by leaps and bounds. High-end communities (and high-end shopping areas), as well as middle-class communities (and middle-class 7-Elevens), are now filling the area. Fortunately for us cowboys at heart, large (very large) parts of the Estates are still rural, still untamed, and still look and feel like the wild, wild West!

Tin City

Tin City is a less expensive and more casual version of the other shopping and dining areas of Naples. The area was named for the corrugated tin roofs that topped all its original buildings. Today, like Goodland, Tin City is a honky-tonk waterside area. It contains boutiques, restaurants, shops, water-based activities, and a winery. The shops sell an eclectic collection of merchandise including monkey bread (try it, you'll like it). Many say that Tin City still sports the charm of old Florida. I guess Old Florida must must have had a lot of honky-tonk.

The dockside area is still covered by a tin roof (that is now red), one of the seven original tin-roofed buildings that still survive. The physical layout of Tin City, as well as its honky-tonk atmosphere attracts several diverse types of crowds, including young people, artists, tourists, winos (it does, after all house a winery), as well as my favorite crowd of all, retired hippies (some of whom are still winos). There is also a plaque at the 11th street entrance that supplies both a little Tin City history and a little more honky-tonk.

Tin City Historical Plaque

> **NOTES ON THE MEANING OF LIFE**—Honky-tonk can mean three things: a) a bar that provides country music, b) the style of music played in these establishments, and c) the type of piano used to play this music.

Tin City is a fun place to visit. It is, as I said, less expensive and more casual that most of the rest of Naples and has an atmosphere that is unmatched in all of Collier County. Except, maybe, at Goodland.

The Airport

Southwest Florida International Airport is the commercial airport serving Naples and surrounding areas. It serves over 10,000,000 airline passengers per year. Since I picked up and/or dropped off most of those passengers (Editor's Note: Some, not most.), I can supply some knowledgeable information about Naples' local aerodrome.

Southwest Florida Regional Airport (RSW) opened on May 14, 1983, as an alternative to the older and smaller Page Field (FMY), which still operates thirteen miles to the northwest. As Southwest Florida grew, so did the airport's name. In 1993, it was renamed Southwest Florida International Airport. The airports IATA (International Air Transport Association) designation was *not* changed, so it is still known as RSW.

While RSW is a relatively modern airport, it does contain some bygone history. One day, I was driving on the north side of the runway and noticed a plethora of roads, parking lots, and passenger pickup lanes, all strangely and completely abandoned. They were in the middle of nowhere and there were no buildings in sight! The area presented such a bizarre look that I expected to hear the Rod Serling intoning, "For your examination, a dazed and confused Uber driver thinks he is driving through a modern airport, but he is traveling through another dimension, a dimension not only of sight and sound but of mind. A journey into a wondrous land whose boundaries are that of imagination. That's the signpost up ahead—your next stop, the RSW Zone!"

Where was I? And what was this place?

I had to find out, so when I had returned to our dimension (i.e., that night), I searched the internet and discovered that I had been wandering past the airport's old passenger terminal (and its adjacent roads, parking lots, and pickup lanes). The old terminal building was demolished when the current terminal, which is located south of the runway, opened in 2005. For some reason, the old roads, parking lots, and passenger pickup lanes weren't removed; they were just left, well, lying there.

RSW has a Jekyll-Hyde personality. In the winter, it is a bustling airport, packed with passengers, cars, airplanes, and Uber drivers. In the summer however, the airport is far less hectic and everyone gets to enjoy some quiet time!

Fortunately, RSW is well designed for any season. The arrival/departure lanes have ample space to pick up and drop off passengers, there is ample parking, the walk to the gates is short, TSA checks don't take too long, and the rental car desks are near the arrivals area. In addition,

Red Flame Enjoying some Quiet Time at the Airport

almost all airport personnel are friendly and courteous. The only exception is the airport police force. When they catch an innocent motorist exceeding 15 mph in the arrival or departure lanes, they become downright ungentlemanly, especially if you are caught twice in one day. (Believe me, I know!)

On April 3, 2020, RSW was the site of the Great Fire of Naples. That day, 3,991 cars that were parked on a fifteen-acre grass rental car overflow lot south of the terminal building burned to the ground, along with their gasoline, lead acid batteries, magnesium engine parts, and toxic plastic. The fire caused almost $100 million in damage. Grass didn't grow on the overflow lot for over a year. Perhaps the burning gasoline, lead acid batteries, magnesium engine parts, and toxic plastic had something to do with that. The fire was ultimately ruled to be accidental, although parking cars with hot catalytic converters in tall grass seems more negligent than accidental to me. The fire can still be viewed on YouTube. The 3,991 burned out carcasses were not removed for six months.

CHAPTER 2

Uber and Me—The Backstory

THE HISTORY OF HUMAN TRANSPORTATION AND UBER TECHNOLOGIES, INC.

From the dawn of time, man has sought out ways to temporarily travel from one place to another at a pace faster than walking. Over the years, horses, camels, canoes, boats, dogsleds, wagons, rickshaws, and sedan chairs were all used for this purpose, which became known as transient personal transport (i.e., unscheduled, individual travel).

Transient personal transport changed profoundly when the internal combustion engine began to power trains, boats, and, most importantly, automobiles. Autos quickly became not only the most popular method of personal transport, but the symbol of the twentieth century.

The rise of the automobile spawned the taxicab industry, which, for over a hundred years, was the most common, economical, and efficient method of transient personal transport.

Unfortunately, the taxi industry began to change. Taxicabs became dirty, unreliable, and expensive, and their use plummeted.

> **NOTES ON THE MEANING OF LIFE**—The reason for the decline of the taxi industry is complex, but the major causes are the limitation by cities of the number of cabs allowed to operate and the low (sometimes nonexistent) standards required of both cars and drivers.

Fortunately for transient, personal transportees, in January 2010 Uber Technologies, Inc. initiated the Uber ride-sharing service. This service allows a passenger, via the Uber passenger app and a smartphone, to "ring" the nearest Uber driver, who can accept the call and quickly and efficiently pick up the passenger and transport him to his destination. The Uber concept quickly became immensely popular.

> **NOTES ON THE MEANING OF LIFE**—The proper noun Uber (like the proper nouns Xerox and Google) has already transmogrified into a verb. Today, people can Uber home to Xerox a document and Google the news!

The ideas and procedures introduced by Uber were well thought out, efficient and effective, highly effective.[14] Uber (and its main rival, Lyft) quickly dominated the transient personal transportation market and became the best way for an individual to, on demand, transiently travel from one place to another in a private automobile.

A passenger almost anywhere in America (and many other

---

14   After the introduction of Uber, the number of daily taxicab rides in New York City dropped from 500,000 to less than 250,000. The price of a taxi medallion dropped from \$1,000,000 to \$130,000.

countries) can request an Uber ride and be whisked to his destination in a private automobile by a friendly and efficient Uber driver. According to a 2018 survey, thirty-six percent of all U.S. adults use ride-sharing services like Uber and Lyft.

NOTES ON THE MEANING OF LIFE—Its Teutonic name notwithstanding, Uber has nothing to do with Germany, although they do operate there.

HELPFUL HINTS FOR UBER PASSENGERS

Since over a third of you reading this book use Uber and/or Lyft, here are a few tips to improve your "Uber Experience":

1. Be ready at the arrival time shown on the Uber app. Remember, if a ride doesn't begin within three minutes of the driver's arrival, a waiting fee is charged.

2. Smoking, gambling, spitting, drug use,[15] foul language, heavy petting, and the consumption of alcohol are all prohibited in Uber vehicles. If you feel the need, ask the driver to pull over.

3. The front passenger seat is, by definition, available to passengers who want to sit in the front seat![16]

4. If you would like the driver to change the air conditioner setting or the radio volume, just (nicely)

---

15   The rule against drug use does not apply to the use of prescription Coumadin, Lipitor, Cialis, Prozac, Simvastatin, Lisinopril, Insulin, or Synthroid.

16   During the Covid pandemic, Uber drivers were instructed by Uber not to allow passengers in the front seat.

ask the driver. Many drivers, like me, offer a wide selection of music, including jazz, easy listening, Gregorian chants (just kidding) and classical.

5. If you live in a gated community, **either text the Uber driver the gate code** or **call the gate** so the Uber driver can gain entry!

6. And most importantly! When being picked up in a crowd, such as at the arrivals area at an airport, check the photo of the Uber driver's car on the Uber app and **vigorously wave** at the driver as soon as he arrives. Continue **waving** until he sees you. Remember, approaching Uber drivers only know the passenger's first name and won't be able to determine which person in the crowd is their passenger!

AN INQUISITIVE UBER DRIVER'S TRICKS OF THE TRADE

When I started driving, I wasn't satisfied with my passenger count or my earnings. As I talked shop with a few fellow Uber drivers who happened to be my passengers (yup, Uber drivers use Uber!), I learned a few of their tricks of the Uber trade.

I began my tour as an Uber driver just as Covid began its "tour" of America when the demand for rides was low (sometimes non-existent). Thus, I also had a lot of time to also create a few of my own tricks of the Uber trade. Here are some I used.

The Double Whammy—Avoiding Other Uber Drivers by Using the Uber Passenger App

Uber Technologies "rings" the driver nearest the customer requesting the ride, so I tried to find a way to be as far away from other Uber drivers as possible.

The Uber driver's app does not provide the location of other Uber drivers. However, the Uber *passenger* app does, so I started using that app to see where other Uber drivers were trolling (driving around waiting to be called for a pickup) and I trolled elsewhere. This technique was moderately successful.

Using Online Statistical Stuff

Since I wanted to be near the most potential customers, I wanted to find the areas of Collier County that had the densest (numerically, not intellectually) population. I was able to do this by downloading a few County population density maps from the internet.

When I started trolling these densely populated areas, my passenger count increased only slightly. I didn't understand why until I noticed (via the Uber passenger app) that other Uber drivers were just as smart as I was and were trolling the same areas! The areas with the highest population density also had the highest Uber driver density!

Then I remembered that there were two areas in Collier County that were rapidly developing. They didn't have a high population density yet because they were so large, but they contained a lot of (widely dispersed) potential passengers, were rapidly growing, and (as I determined via the Uber passenger app) were populated by almost no Uber drivers!

The areas were the southwest fringe of the populated part

of Naples (near the intersection of Collier Boulevard and Tamiami Trail) and the Estates. By trolling these fringe areas, I figured I had a good chance to be called for a ride.

I didn't have much luck near Collier Boulevard and Tamiami Trail but hit the jackpot by trolling the fringe of the Estates. I was called for a lot of rides and, since the Estates is so large and is far away from everywhere else, almost every ride included a Pickup Premium (See d below: The Pickup Premium Hoedown/Slowdown) and was a long-duration ride.

Picking Up a Few Pennies Via a Few Quirks in the Uber App

I also uncovered a few quirks in the Uber driver app that I exploited to increase my earnings. The increase was minimal, but I enjoyed the adventure of gaming the system.

First, I learned not to end a ride (on the Uber driver's app) as soon as I arrived, but to wait until all passengers and their belongings were out of the car. This extended the ride a few seconds and increased that ride's earnings by a few cents.[17]

Another quirk involves the charge for waiting time. If an Uber driver waits more than three minutes, the passenger is charged, and the Uber driver is paid a waiting time premium. I discovered the waiting time clock begins ticking when I got to within a few blocks of the pickup point. Hence, I always slowed down the last few blocks to maximize any

---

17 The Uber formula for charging a passenger is extremely complicated and constantly changing. Basically, the fare is based on the ride's duration and length. However, many other charges can be added (such as a pickup premium, waiting time, surge hours, etc.). The formula for the part of a passenger charge paid to a driver is even more complicated, but generally a driver retains from about 40 percent (for short trips) to about 70 percent (for long trips) of the total fare.

potential waiting time premium. A few more cents!

The Pickup Premium Hoedown/Slowdown

One final legal but certainly unethical trick I used was the Pickup Premium Hoedown/Slowdown. Uber drivers are usually not compensated for the time and distance to pick up a passenger; their time and distance compensation begins once the passenger is picked up. However, there is an exception to this rule. If the Uber app estimates it will take longer than a local limit (eleven minutes in Naples) to pick up a passenger *and* it does, in fact, take longer than that limit, the driver is paid a Pickup Premium; time and distance compensation begins when the driver has been driving for eleven minutes.

If a ride qualifies for a Pickup Premium, but the driver arrives in less than eleven minutes, no Pickup Premium is paid to the driver. Therefore, by driving "very cautiously" for the first eleven minutes of a ride that is eligible for a Pickup Premium, I earned a few more cents.

I felt bad whenever employing a Pickup Premium Slowdown, but, again, I found it challenging to game the system. Of course, I now realize the error of my ways. Therefore, to salve both my Flower Child and Cowboy conscience, I would like to formally apologize to all my passengers whose pickups took longer than eleven minutes. My bad, sorry pardner.

The Gratuity Maximization Strategy

I (like every other red-blooded American who earns tips) always looked for ways to increase my tip income. Of course,

I employed all "normal" tip increasing actions: I was always polite; I always made sure passengers agreed with my choice or volume of music (most didn't like the Gregorian chants); I always asked if the ambient atmospheric ambiance was adequate (i.e., Is the A/C okay?); and I always offered both Android and Apple phone charging.

I discovered another significant way to increase gratuity income: quickly discover whether a passenger wants to talk during the trip or prefers quiet time. Sometimes, this was easy to figure out; some passengers began talking the minute they entered the car and continued chatting until they were dropped off. They preferred conversation over silence. (See Talkative Ted, below.) On the other hand, some passengers began reading, writing, talking on the phone, or working on a computer as soon as they got into the car. In these cases, I knew silence was golden.

If it was difficult to tell whether a passenger was interested in conversation or not, I had to draw on all my life experiences to determine whether I should be my usual loquacious self or shut the f*** up. (I was usually successful in making this determination.)

Many passengers complimented me on my conversations and a few even complimented me on my silence.

> **NOTES ON THE MEANING OF LIFE**—Passengers who compliment are generally good tippers!

Giving Back—A Reverse Gratuity Program

To both distinguish myself from other Uber drivers and to sustain my Hippie instinct to "give back," I regularly distributed reverse gratuities to my passengers. On Christmas Day, I gave each passenger a gold (well, golden) Sacajawea dollar coin. On Robert (aka Robbie) Burns Day (January 25), I gave passengers a small package of Walker's shortbread. I intended to give my female passengers[18] a rose on Valentine's Day, but I didn't look for roses until the last minute and their price was too high.

During the Covid pandemic, I offered my passengers small bottles of hand sanitizer. Needless to say, they went like hotcakes!

THE EFFECTIVE USE OF MILLINERY

From the beginning of time, all drivers wore hats. Whether it was camel hacks in ancient Egypt; sedan chair operators in eighteenth century China; or personal chauffeurs such as Rochester, Hoke, and Kato, they all sported distinctive headgear.

In keeping with this fine tradition instituted by my illustrious predecessors, I always made it a point to wear a hat while driving. In fact, I wore two: a white Panama Hat in the summer and a herringbone Gatsby Cabbie Cap (more than appropriate, I thought![19]) in the winter.

Clothes may make the man, but hats make the driver!

I CAN HEAR MUSIC

18   Probably a civil rights violation, but I'll be damned if I am ever going to give a rose to a guy.

19   As shown on the book cover.

Friedrich Nietzsche said, "Without music, life would be a mistake." Well, Fred would have made a great Uber driver because driving for Uber without music is also a mistake. I always made it a point, both in my Uber bio and in conversations with passengers, to let passengers know that all types of music are available. I was surprised at how much passengers appreciated the music of their choice! Most requests were for Classic Rock or Adult Contemporary, but many liked Jimmy Buffet (well, Naples is a beach community and a Margaritaville resort is being built in Fort Myers Beach).

If I didn't receive a request from a passenger, I usually played Easy Listening or the SiriusXM 40s station. I found that as I got older, I started listening to my parents' music. However, when I drove other lapsed hippies, I always kept a Hard Rock CD handy. Nothing like roaring down I-75 with Ozzy screaming Paranoia.[20]

YEAH, YEAH, YEAH, SO HOW MUCH DOES AN UBER DRIVER MAKE?

Who knows! Earnings vary by season, by day of the week, by time of day, by how long and when a driver is willing to work, and whether Uber Technologies has cut driver fares again. Drivers I know earned from $250[21] to $1,300 per week, depending on the above variables.

---

20   Black Sabbath Paranoia. Ozzy Osbourne, lead singer.
21   Keep in mind that about 20 to 25 percent of Uber earnings must be used to buy gas. (In 2022, this percentage rose to 35–40%.)

CHAPTER 3

Lore, Legends, and a Few Fun Facts Vis-à-vis Naples

YE OLDE NUDIST COLONY

I'll start this chapter with the most interesting (and most titillating) story that I heard during my tenure as an Uber driver, the story of Naples' long-lost nudist colony.

The story begins at Whippoorwill Lane, a short, nondescript, dead-end in the northeastern part of Naples that extends south from Pine Ridge Road and runs for about a mile. At the end of the lane is a wooded lake that is now surrounded by numerous buildings.

During my travels, several passengers told me that before the buildings were constructed, there was an informal nudist colony on the shores of the lake. The colony was not licensed or sanctioned: it was just a few friends (assuredly close ones) who liked to let it all hang out. They would lounge around and swim in the lake, sans clothing. One passenger recounted that when she was young, she often walked around the lake (when it was unoccupied, so she said) and saw that the colonists had placed used furniture, suitable for lounging, all around the lake.

Another passenger told me that before the foliage lining I-75 matured, a lot of the colony's activities, including au natural jet skiing on the lake, were visible from the highway! I hope the skiers used enough sunscreen! Imagine getting a severely sunburned . . . well, you know!

I was curious as to whether any similar facilities still operate in Naples. After some cunctation, I initiated hands on research, including intrusive personal (but safe) interaction with both sexes. As a result of my intercourse with numerous sources (including a sexagenarian), I learned that two similar facilities are still more than titularly servicing Naples, but it is unclear whether any penal violations are involved. I could reveal more, but my lips are sealed!

ON GOLDEN (GATE) POND (CANAL)

One afternoon, I drove an elderly native Neapolitan who told me that, when he was young, he and his friends swam in Naples Bay and ate raw clams they had dug from the sand. Things are different today. Naples Bay is far too polluted for swimming, and anyone who eats a raw clam freshly dug from the bay's shoreline (if they can find one) is courting botulism.

I asked how the bay got so polluted and my passenger told me the pollution was caused by the completion of the Golden Gate Canal in the late 1960s. I checked his story and he was right. The canal, which is about twenty miles long, drains a vast area of Collier County and funnels 411 million gallons of water (and anything and everything in it) into the bay *every day*! The canal destroyed the saltwater wetlands (fka swamps) next to the bay and killed most of the neighboring marine life. On the positive side, the Golden Gate Canal System is now a freshwater fisherman's dream and, oh yes, recently the county has begun investigating ways to undo the canal's damage.

SOPHISTICATES AT THE GATE (AND THEIR CODES)

There are over 120 gated communities in Naples and, as a friendly and hard-working Uber driver, I have picked up or dropped off passengers in almost all of them. The gates at most of these communities have a living, breathing security guard who confirms visitors' identities and destinations. Some communities, however, dispense with the human guard. Their gates consist of only a keypad and, of course, a gate. At "Keypad Only" gates, a visitor must type a gate code into the keypad before the gates will swing (or lift) open.

During my stint as an Uber driver, I was given, and used, almost every gate code in town. However, I am thinking of changing my procedures. If I don't make enough money from the sale of this book, I'm thinking of publishing all the gate codes in a book directed at the, shall we say, less fortunate among us (i.e., burglars, ex-spouses, disinherited children, grifters, and addicts). I am certain the book will sell like hotcakes!

ELYSIAN FIELDS

Near the periphery of Collier County is a heaven on Earth, especially if you consider yourself an old cowboy or a back-to-nature hippie. Collier's heaven on Earth is the 13,000-acre Audubon Corkscrew Swamp Sanctuary (as good a name as any for a heaven; well, sanctuary is — I'm not too sure about

Corkscrew and Swamp). The Sanctuary is about twenty miles northeast of the City of Naples, right in the middle of nowhere, exactly where heaven should be. It provides a view of nature in its original pristine condition, untouched by human hands, except for the miles of rustic boardwalks, which were presumably built by human hands. The boardwalks go over ponds and streams; through thickets of plants and trees; around, over, and sometimes through groups of alligators; and past the largest remaining stand of old-growth virgin bald cypress trees in the world. The Sanctuary contains all sorts of extraordinary wildlife and vegetation. Reservations are purportedly required but, since there is rarely a human in sight in the sanctuary, I don't see how the ticket policy is enforced.

P.S. Heaven is seasonal. Avoid visiting the sanctuary in the summer; it is hot, the swamp is dry, and the animals are all hiding.

THE MEANING OF IMMOKALEE

The name Immokalee is omnipresent in Naples. Immokalee Road is the main east-west artery in the northern part of Naples; many local businesses bear the moniker; and there is a town about a half-hour northeast of Naples called Immokalee (the original Miccosukee Indian name of the area was, in English, Gopher Ridge). Since the name is so popular and so strange, I wanted to find out where it came from and what it meant. I often asked passengers if they knew anything about the word. One passenger thought it sounded Hawaiian. Another said it sounded like the noise someone makes when they are choking to death.

My interest was piqued, so I turned to the internet and found out Immokalee means "my home" in Mikasuki (sounds Japanese), which is the Miccosukee's (sounds Thai) language.[22] So, when residents of Immokalee say, "Immokalee is Immokalee," they know what they're talking about.

WHY SO MANY PLACES HAVE *HAMMOCK* IN THEIR NAME

When I first got to Naples, I noticed that many place names contained the word *hammock*. There is a Rattlesnake Hammock Road, a community called Cedar Hammock, a club called Hammock Bay, and even a paddling trail called Royal Palm Hammock. I knew Southerners tended to be laid back, but I couldn't imagine they needed a hammock wherever they went. Of course, that is because I thought *hammock* only meant "a bed made of canvas or rope mesh and suspended by cords at the ends." However, after I had been in Florida for a while, I learned that *hammock* has another meaning; "a small natural hill, usually in a swamp." So, it looks like Southerners are not so lazy after all; they just have a lot of small natural hills in their swamps.

EXPLOSIONS AT THE HIGH SCHOOL

Lely Resort is a 25,000-acre community[23] located near Lely High School. Construction of Lely Resort began in the 1970s. Several passengers told me that when they were students at Lely High during that time, their classes were

---

22   Mikasuki is currently the native language of 290 Floridians. I don't think I ever drove any of them.

23   Actually, Lely Resort is a "community of communities." that contains thirty-nine sub communities.

often interrupted by loud explosions: the blasting that was necessary to construct Lely Resort.

PARLEZ-VOUS FRANCAIS?

I don't know much French. However, three words of French I do know are *mer*, which means sea (I'm a Moody Blues fan and one of their albums is *Sur La Mer*—On the Sea), *chateau*, which means castle (I'm also an Elton John fan and one of his albums is *Honky Chateau*—Honky Castle), and *mère*, which means mother (I'm also a fan of French expletives). So, imagine my surprise when I dropped off a passenger in Pelican Bay at a community called Chateaumêre! I think the developers meant to call the community Chateaumer (Castle by the Sea), but since they were Americans whose knowledge of French was limited to French toast, French fries, and French dressing, they called it Chateaumêre, Mom's Castle (or worse, Mother Castle) in error!

MEL'S DINER

Everyone knows Mel's Diner from the old CBS sitcom *Alice*. But the real Mel's diner is in Naples, at three separate locations. Mel's is an upscale (what in Naples is not upscale?) diner that serves great food. A passenger, who worked at Mel's, told me that the three diners were originally owned by a family company but, due to some intra-family quarreling, the organization split up and each diner was transferred to a different family member. The passenger also told me that, while all the diners offer equally superb meals, the food at the Collier Boulevard Mel's is more equally superb than the food at the other Mel's. (Yup, that's the one he worked at.) So, if you are ever in Naples, stop at the Collier Boulevard Mel's! (Author's Note: Say, "Hi" to Mel, Alice, and Flo. They still work there.) (Editor's Note: No, they don't!)

LOST NAPLES

Old Timer passengers told me many stories about the Naples of bygone days; a Naples that, today, exists only as a happy memory. Every time one of these passengers finished one of their stories, they always sighed and murmured, "It's a shame things had to change."

Old Roads

Due to the rapid growth of Naples, almost every road has been expanded, modified, or extended. Elderly (and some not so elderly) passengers often told me of the "old" roads in Naples. One passenger told me of how Immokalee used to be a dirt road from Airport Pulling east. Another said that there used to be vast groves of orange trees where some of Livingston Road now stands. A third told me that the intersection of Golden Gate Parkway and Airport Pulling Road was the worst intersection in the county and that it always took at least twenty minutes to get through the traffic light there. He further added that on the northwest corner of the intersection was a huge farmer's market that, in season, allowed customers to roam the strawberry patch and pick their own strawberries.

Most of the "old" roads are long gone, but occasionally, if you look carefully, you can find snippets of them still in use alongside their modern counterparts. Parts of "old" Livingston Road can be seen on the east side of modern Livingston Road just north of Pine Ridge Road. Likewise, parts of "old" Tamiami Trail can also be seen on the east side of the modern road, also just north of Pine Ridge. There is also an old road (39 Street SW) that runs parallel to Collier Boulevard at Golden Gate Parkway. I tried to find out if that road was "old" Collier Boulevard, but no one seemed to know. (It sure looks like it was!)

There is one "old" road that is more difficult to detect. An elderly passenger explained to me that Logan Boulevard and Santa Barbara Boulevard used to be separate roads and did not connect with each other. They both ended (Logan from the north and Santa Barbara from the south) at Green Boulevard, about a tenth of a mile apart. I drove the road and was able to uncover each road's original course.

If you are traveling south on Logan Boulevard, shortly after you cross Pine Ridge Road, there is a slight curve to the right just before the Logan turns into Santa Barbara Boulevard. Prior to the curve and straight ahead is another road that was, but is no longer, connected to Logan Boulevard. This "straight ahead" road, now called Logan Court, used to be the end of Logan Boulevard just before it ended at Green Boulevard. Northbound Santa Barbara Boulevard also ended at Green Boulevard about five hundred feet west of the intersection of "old" Logan Boulevard (now Logan Court). To make the Logan Boulevard/Santa Barbara Boulevard connection, Logan Court was cut off from Logan Boulevard and Logan Boulevard was curved to the right and rerouted into Santa Barbara Boulevard. This created today's thoroughfare (or Boulevardfare) of Logan/Santa Barbara Boulevard while the cut-off portion of "old" Logan Boulevard was renamed Logan Court, which is now a short dead-end street.

Vanished Railroad Tracks

At one time there were railroad tracks everywhere in Naples. Even Marco Island had a railroad station called Collier City (the original name of the city of Marco Island). Originally, tracks extended south from Tallahassee all the way to Everglades City. In Naples, they ran south along Goodlette-Frank Road until they split just north of Vanderbilt Beach Road. The main line veered slightly east and continued south to Everglades City, while a spur continued down Goodlette-Frank Road to its two terminuses in Naples. One terminus was the railroad station and the other was where Marine Max Naples now stands near Tin City. The line now terminates in North Naples, near Wiggins Pass Road. Almost all the old tracks have been removed, but parts of the old rail system can still be seen if you know where to look.

One of the best places to look, at least for the track bed (the tracks themselves are long gone), is on the west side of Goodlette-Frank Road, north of Vanderbilt Beach Road. Most of the original track bed is covered by the southbound lanes of Goodlette-Frank, but if you look carefully on the west shoulder of the road, you can still discern long, flat, six-foot-wide sections of grass that once held railroad tracks.

Sugar Sands

Several older passengers told me that when they were young, there were vast expanses of sugar sands in and around Naples. They told me of walking or riding their horses, bikes, or ATVs through seas of sugar sands. A few areas of sugar sands still exist, but most have been covered by pavement, vegetation, or buildings.

> **NOTES ON THE MEANING OF LIFE**—Sugar Sands are a fine silt, composed of ultrafine mineral sand and organic granules.

WHAT'S WITH THE DEAD TREES ALONG THE HIGHWAYS?

In the 1930s, Lee and Collier Counties were concerned that the then-new development in the area would disrupt the normal drainage of the land. They were afraid that excess water would pool and endanger local plant and animal life.

So, the city fathers devised Plan A: import a ton (actually many, many tons) of Australian Melaleuca trees, which absorb a lot of water, and plant them everywhere. In theory, they would keep the land dry and save the local animal and plant life. Unfortunately, the two counties didn't consider the theory/practice paradox.

> **NOTES ON THE MEANING OF LIFE**—The Theory/ Practice Paradox states that, in theory, theory and practice are the same, but in practice, they're not!

In theory, the imported trees would absorb water, but in practice, they absorbed too much of it. Many native trees (and probably a few native animals) began dying of thirst! In 1984, the National Park Service was forced to implement Plan B: murder the Aussie bastards! Since then, in many areas, including the stretch of I-75 on the way to Fort Myers, Australian Melaleuca trees have been intentionally poisoned and killed by the state.

THE REALM OF RESTAURANTS

Minnesota may be the land of ten thousand lakes, but Naples is the realm of ten thousand restaurants.[24] Since it would be impossible to list and review all of them, I suggest you try each one to find your favorites.

---

24   There are about one thousand restaurants in Collier County.

> **NOTES ON THE MEANING OF LIFE**—The Minnesota Department of Natural Resources defines a lake as a still body of water of more than ten acres. Pursuant to that definition, Minnesota has 11,842 lakes.

While Naples has restaurants all over the place, most of them are concentrated in six areas: the city's two downtowns, Tin City, Marco Island, Golden Gate City,[25] and along the Tamiami Trail.

Normally, restaurants are grouped into two categories: Fine Dining and Casual Dining. However, I have added two additional categories: Godawfully Expensive (but Godawfully Good) Dining (a nod to the immense wealth of the diners in Naples) and the Best Local Hangouts (a nod to all the locals (and tourists) who just want to "hang out.")

Here are a few of my passengers' (and my) favorite eateries in each category and a few thoughts on each.

Godawfully Expensive (but Godawfully Good) Dining

Ocean Prime—Billed an American, seafood, steak restaurant, it has the best (and highest-priced) seafood in Naples. It also has a very sophisticated (but almost show-offy) atmosphere.

Truluck's—Spectacular seafood, steaks, and prices. Atmosphere is a notch more realistic than Ocean Prime.

---

25 Not to be confused with Golden Gate Estates. Golden Gate City is an almost perfect two-mile by two-mile square (comprising four square miles) area just east of central Naples, while Golden Gate Estates is farther east (and north, and south) and is almost twenty-five times the size (geographically) of Golden Gate City. To confuse things even further, the main road in Golden Gate City is Golden Gate Parkway while the main road to and in Golden Gate Estates is Golden Gate Boulevard.

The Grill at the (Vanderbilt Beach Boulevard) Ritz-Carlton—Everything at The Grill is great and everything at The Grill is expensive, but it is the classiest (without going overboard) restaurant in Naples. Furthermore, all the hotel's/restaurant's personnel (especially the female gate guard, who welcomes all Uber drivers with a hearty "Hi, honey!") are the friendliest around. Fortunately, The Grill offers a few specials to (slightly) ease the financial pain of eating there. Dining at The Grill is expensive, (But the sauces are free, so load up on the Béarnaise) but if you want to impress someone, The Grill is the place to go!

The Capital Grille—This is a restaurant that really believes in truth in advertising. Their name says it all. You will need capital to eat at this grill. It is as good (and as expensive) as any restaurant in Naples, but far more importantly, the parking lot at The Capital Grille always has the largest collection of fine (and not-so-fine) cars in town. They are generally owned by elderly men who are trying to attract women by openly displaying their small coúpes and junkers.

The Pub (Naples)—This restaurant is in the Mercato, a genuinely nice, upscale shopping/dining/office/residential mall in the northern part of Naples. This restaurant is part of a nationwide chain and its prices are reasonable (very reasonable for the Mercato). The Pub serves mostly British fare with few American favorites thrown in. Although good British food is usually a contradiction in terms, the food at The Pub is rather good. After 7 p.m., the collection of fine cars outside The Pub sometimes rivals those at The Capital Grille.

> **NOTES ON THE MEANING OF LIFE**—*Mercato* means market in Italian.

Osteria Tulia & Bay Tulia—Osteria Tulia is one of the best Italian restaurants in Naples. Fortunately, Bar Tulia shares the same owner, the same kitchen, and the same caliber of food with Osteria Tulia, but Bar Tulia has a livelier (i.e., younger) atmosphere.

Sea Salt—A run-of-the-mill good-food, high-price restaurant, except that, unlike all other restaurants, Sea Salt offers its patrons almost one hundred distinct types of salt to put on their French fries. Many of my passengers liked eating at Sea Salt, but none of them understood the salt thing! P.S. It is reported that all Sea Salt employees have high blood pressure!

The French—Great French food for people who ordinarily don't like French food, like me.

Fine (i.e., not that expensive) Dining

Bleu Provence—A nice little country French restaurant in a nice little country part of Naples (Crayton Cove). Everything at Bleu Provence is wonderful, except for the onion soup, which is rather ordinary.

Tommy Bahamas—A nice "theme" restaurant. The food is good and so is the atmosphere. The large sliding glass doors are always kept open, so even when you are dining inside, you are dining al fresco! There is a Tommy Bahama store inside the restaurant, so if your order takes too long to arrive, you can pick up some swimwear or casual clothing while waiting.

The Continental—My (and a few of my passengers') favorite, which makes The Continental the best restaurant in town. Their usual prices are high, which would normally place this restaurant in the Godawfully Expensive (but Godawfully Good) category, but I am placing it here because they always (even in the winter) have dining specials that bring their prices back to sea level. At The Continental, guests can dine outside, dine inside, or dine in tents straight out of *Lawrence of Arabia*. As well as being a Fine Dining restaurant, The Continental is also a fine drinking restaurant as they serve a multitude of specialty drinks!

Campiello—Campiello is owned by the same people as The Continental. The food is just as good (and just as expensive), but they don't have as many specials. Campiello also doesn't have any Arabian tents, but you can dine in a nice faux greenhouse or on the patio out back.

Casual Dining

Mino's—Mino's is the best casual dining restaurant in Naples. It is also one of the least expensive (for Naples). Mino's is essentially a pizzeria, but it is a pizzeria on steroids! They have all kinds of great pizza as well as many tasty entrees and appetizers. Before I came to Florida, I asked a friend (who owns a great Italian restaurant and has a winter home in Naples) for the best restaurant (not Italian restaurant, just restaurant) in Naples. Without batting an eye, he said Mino's. (P.S. they also have great gelato!)

Snook Inn—The Snook Inn is on Marco Island and is probably Marco's number one tourist restaurant. Fortunately, the food and ambiance at Snook are better than the food and ambiance of most tourist restaurants. Snook has live music in the afternoon and in the evening and you can dine inside, outside, or at the tiki bar.

Brooks Burgers (technically, Brooks Gourmet Burgers and Dogs)—One of the benefits of being a hamburger lover and an author is that you can include your favorite burger joint in the book even if it might not qualify on its own. Well, Brooks Burgers is my favorite burger joint, but it certainly qualifies on its own (TripAdvisor rates them the number two hamburger restaurant in America). They serve over twenty hamburger combinations, including a burger served on a glazed doughnut (no, I never had one), along with a potpourri of other dishes. Brooks Burgers also has a full (and rather large) bar.

The first time I was at Brooks Burgers, I was helped by a very polite, but young maître d'. After we had an extended conversation about the food business, I commented on the airplane photos displayed throughout the restaurant.

"The airplane photos are a nice touch," I said. "The owner must be an airplane enthusiast."

"You're right," Todd Brooks replied, "I am."

Texas Tony's Rib and Brew House, Texas Roadhouse, and any other restaurant with "Texas" or "Rib" in their name— good ribs, good chicken, good beer. 'Nuff said.

Napoli-by-the Bay—All ex-New Yorkers know it is impossible to find real New York pizza anywhere south of the Mason-Dixon line. Fortunately, there is an exception in Naples. Napoli-by-the-Bay (five, soon to be six locations) is a pizzeria that serves the real thing. While other local pizzerias come awfully close (Rosedale Pizza and New York Pizza and

Pasta come to mind), Napoli-by-the Bay has the real thing.

Three60 Market (Café and Wine Shop)—Three60 Market is one of the strangest, yet one of the most enjoyable casual eateries in Naples. It is not exactly a market, nor is not exactly a café or a wine shop. It is best described as a delicatessen on steroids where customers can either pick up food (and wine) to eat (and drink) at home or sit down and eat (and drink) on premises (either indoors or al fresco). Three60, which is sited in a large, timeworn house next to a canal, offers a wide variety of gastronomic treats; standard deli fare, gourmet sandwiches, soups, burgers, chicken, and numerous other tasty dishes that are rarely found elsewhere.

In addition to food, Three60 market also offers wine. A good friend is a ~~wino~~ wine connoisseur who tells me that Three60 sells quality wines at reasonable prices. In fact, Three60 got its name because they only mark up each bottle of wine $3.60. And best of all, diners can buy one or more bottles of wine to enjoy while dining on premises and can take home any wine they don't consume!

Celebration Park—Right next door (actually, across the canal, less than a block's walk) from Three60 Market is Celebration Park, another Naples dining experience, where younger, less affluent, but more fun-loving diners meet to greet and eat. (Some also tweet!) Celebration Park comes in several pieces. There is a large outdoor bar (with live music); numerous tables, suitable for use in eating and drinking; and about eight to ten different food trucks. These trucks are not the run-of-the-mill roach coaches. Oh, no! They are clean, airy and offer a wide variety of pedestrian and exotic foods, such as Mexican, Kobe beef burgers, gyros, duck burgers, lobster rolls, and Asian specialties, among others. Oh, I almost forgot, did I mention there is also a large outdoor bar?

While dropping off and picking up passengers at Celebration Park I noticed something very attention-grabbing. The women who frequent Celebration Park are all very pretty!

Seed to Table—I saved the best in this category for last. While a little pricey (but still casual), Seed to Table is more than a restaurant; it is an entertainment experience. Seed to Table is so distinctive, it must be explained in layers. The first layer is the Seed to Table facility itself. It is a massive, upscale supermarket that has everything you want, everything you need, and everything you never heard of, including six kinds of Scottish Shortbread. Within the supermarket layer are various and sundry restaurants sprinkled all over the place. The final layer is the drinking layer. Along with the restaurants, there is a coffee bar, a wine bar, a beer bar, and an upscale "regular" bar scattered throughout the facility to assure that any thirst, as well as any hunger, can be adequately satiated.

At Seed to Table, a hale and hearty cowboy (like me) can kill his dinner (find a piece of meat at the Seed to Table butcher shop), clean and dress it (select it), cook it over a hot campfire (ask to have it cooked well done), and eat it with his women folk (have it brought to his table). Unfortunately, Seed to Table insists everyone, including cowboys, use their utensils.

Since I am an OG, the live music at Seed to Table sometimes seems a bit loud, but if you are under fifty-five, Seed to Table is the place to be!

During the Covid pandemic, Seed to Table, unlike most

dining emporia, sported a unique welcome sign: "Masks Are Not Required Here."

Local Hangouts

Naples doesn't really have any bad restaurants. However, like all other cities, towns, and villages, it has several "local hangouts" that don't quite attain a Michelin 3-star rating. The "local hangouts" in Naples are all cheap(er), friendly(ier), (more) boisterous, and (lots of) fun places at which to drink (and/or eat). They all have similar (generally high average) food and similar (very average, but numerous) varieties of drinks. While there are many "local hangouts" in Naples, the following two are among the most popular.

Harold's Place Chickee Bar and Grille (motto: "Where Fun Never Sets")—Harold's Place is located on Tamiami Trail about a thousand feet north of Mooring Line Drive (aka 22nd Avenue N.). It shares a parking lot with Fujiyama Steak and Seafood House and The Gulfcoast Inn. In keeping with the tradition of "local hangouts," Harold's drink menu is just as lengthy as their food menu. There is an interesting poem at the end of the food menu that seems to indicate that Harold's was founded in 1991.

Unlike most of its competition, Harold's shares a pool and several Tiki huts with the Gulfcoast Inn. This means that not only can you eat and drink at Harold's, but you can also swim. (It is not clear if swimming fully clothed is permitted.)

North Naples Country Club—Probably the most popular "local hangout" in Naples. This establishment's name is somewhat of a misnomer. The North Naples Country Club is not a country club, nor is it in North Naples; it is in

Naples Park (North Naples is across the street). This eatery is located at Tamiami Trail and 101st Street. It offers above average "local hangout" fare and is (per several passengers) the oldest, continuously operating bar/restaurant in Naples. Several passengers (who were longtime "Country Club" "members") told me that when the club was founded in 1942 when, it had chicken wire "windows" and a dirt floor.

There is a long-standing tradition at the North Naples Country Club that continues to this day. When the bar closes at 2 a.m., an enterprising hot dog vendor parks her cart at the restaurant exit and does a land-office business. As everyone knows, when leaving a bar at 2 a.m. after drinking all night, the second most important thing needed is a hot dog. The first? A restroom.

FABULOUS FOODLESS FUN AND FROLIC

Besides being the realm of the thousand restaurants, Naples is the kingdom of numerous non-food nonpareils. It has a remarkable zoo that is enjoyed even by the few who eschew a zoo.

Naples' zoo offers a boat ride around an island populated solely by monkeys. Zoo visitors can also stand right next to (and photograph) a giraffe. (Author's Note: Giraffes are much taller in real life than they are on television. They can reach eighty feet in height.) (Editor's Note: Giraffe's are from 17-19 feet tall.)

For the horticulturalists and artists among us, Naples also has a 170-acre Botanical Gardens. The gardens contain all sorts of strange looking (and sounding), exotic and interesting plants, including Soapberry trees, Dragon Fruit Cacti, and several real Gumbo Limbos.[26]

During the Christmas season, the gardens outdo itself with Christmas trimmings and decorations, including numerous glass elves, who seem to pop up in every area of the gardens.

Rounding out Naples' fabulous foodless fun and frolic are Collier County's many museums. There are over 20 museums and historic sites in Collier County. The County operates five of them, which are scattered throughout the county. One is in Marco Island (Marco Island Historical Museum); another, a real ranch, is in the northern part of the county (Immokalee Pioneer Museum at Roberts Ranch); and a third is in Everglades City (Museum of the Everglades). The final two, The Naples Depot Museum and The Collier Museum at Government Center are in Naples and East Naples, respectively. All the county museums are fascinating, but more importantly, they are free!

NAPLES' CRÈME DE LA CRÈME

Most cities have a wealthy neighborhood or two, but because many Naples residents are, well, rich, there are many wealthy neighborhoods here. However, the one that takes the Grand Marnier glazed Linzertorte is Port Royal. Port Royal outperforms (in style, beauty, class, and median home value) every other American neighborhood (including Grosse Point, Greenwich, Lattingtown, Atherton, Scarsdale, and Beverly Hills) in its weight class.

One day, while I was on my way to pick up a Port Royal

---

26 The trees, not to be confused with the Gumbo Limbo café on the beach at the Naples Ritz Carlton Hotel or the Gumbo Limbo Nature Center in Boca Raton.

resident, she sent me a text saying, "Alan, when you get to my house, turn left into the third driveway."

NOTES ON THE MEANING OF LIFE—Port Royal was named after the seventeenth century Jamaican city, known for its privateers and smugglers. A few streets in Port Royal still carry names reminiscent of that era, such as Rum Row, Gin Lane, and Galleon Drive.

Port Royal is also one of the oldest neighborhoods in Naples, the site of the town's original fishing village, and the home of the long gone, but storied and glamorous Naples Hotel. The hotel was built in 1889 at the end of 12th Street (formerly Pier Street) between Second Avenue South (now Gordon Drive) and Third Avenue South at 12th Street. Today, the area is occupied by the parking lot behind the Tommy Bahama Restaurant. The first guest to sign the hotel register was Rose Cleveland, sister of President Grover Cleveland.

NOTES ON THE MEANING OF LIFE—In 1924, the cost of staying at the Naples Hotel was $40 to $140 per week!

NAPLES' CRÈME DE LA HOUSE

The most expensive house in Naples is, of course, in Port Royal. It is valued at $42.5 million.[27] If there is adventure in your blood, try to find Naples' finest. It is on Gordon Drive

---

27   As of 2021. Home prices have increased a lot since then.

and has a four-digit address ending in "0."

NAPOLETANI STRAORDINARIO[28]

Naples has more than its share of the rich and famous. This is partially due to its sunny climate, excellent restaurants, safe streets, and friendly residents. But the primary reason for Naples' popularity among the elite is its superlative Uber service. (Editor's Note: Naples' Uber service has nothing to do with its popularity.) (Author's Note: It does too!)

Sean Hannity (whose heart is not troubled), Bob (not Pete) Seger, Larry Bird, Papa John (Schnatter, not Creach or Phillips), Jose Feliciano (who, thanks to Naples' climate, doesn't have to light many fires), Judge Judy (I swear this is the truth), Chaka Khan (who never misses the water), K.C.[29] (who gets down at night!), the late Donna Summer (who, I'm sure still loves to love us), Jane Seymour (who opens her heart to Naples), and the late Enrico Caruso all call or called Naples home. (Of course, the great Caruso was from the other Naples!)

THERE'S A RIOT GOIN' ON

During the Black Lives Matter and Antifa riots that wracked the country in 2020, I was an interested observer and, of course, an Uber driver. Nationwide, the riots lasted months and no one knew if they would ever come to Naples. Some Neapolitans, especially those of us who needed new electronics, were hoping they would. Fortunately, they did!

One day, word on the street was that protestors would be

---

28   Italian for extraordinary Neapolitans.
29   Of Sunshine Band fame.

rioting at the Coastland Center Mall and would burn down the mall after the riot. I drove past the mall to see if I could purloin a few "necessities" before they became charbroiled. Unfortunately, it looked like every police officer and deputy in Florida was staked out at the mall, which was neither touched nor torched.

A few days later, then there were other rumors that rioting would occur at the Best Buy on Pine Ridge Road. I slept in Red Flame outside the store for a few nights (Editor's Note: no, he didn't), hoping to pick up a new TV, a laptop, and a pair of earbuds as soon as the rioting, er, peaceful protesting started. Unfortunately for me, again, nothing happened. Damn, where were Black Lives Matter and Antifa when I needed them??

Fortunately, the "riots" that occurred in Naples were kept to a minimum and were non-hostile. One day, about 180 "defund the police" protestors "politely" marched on Tamiami Trail for a few hours. There was also a two-day protest on Immokalee Road, where about ninety protestors displayed homemade signs and politely chanted anti-Trump slogans for an hour or so before going home.

It could have been worse, however. A lot of the "defund the police" protestors came to Naples from Miami by bus. A passenger, who was employed by the Hyatt Hotel near River Point Island, told me that Sheriff's deputies stopped the busses at the River Point Island Bridge, just outside the City of Naples and confiscated all the knives, firearms, rocks, clubs, nunchucks, shivs, and other weapons the would-be protestors were carrying. Don't you just love the Naples constabulary? The police "defunded" the protestors!

CRIME AND PUNISHMENT

Even considering the mini protests that occurred in Naples, the city is still way behind most other cities when it comes to the crime game. In calendar year 2020, the City of Naples had one murder,[30] two rapes, one robbery, and seven assaults. Violent crimes in Naples are 87 percent lower than the national average, and Naples is the second safest city in Florida.

NOTES ON THE MEANING OF LIFE—Sweetwater, Florida is the safest city.

THE MUTHA OF ALL SPORTS FACILITIES

The residents of Collier County may be chronologically old, but they are also spry, very spry and participate in many active sports[31], golf, tennis and pickleball being the most popular. To accommodate the county's sports-minded, geriatrics, as well as to provide a venue for the sporting needs of the County's 46,329 elementary and high school students, Collier County built a massive sports complex in the eastern part of Naples (near the Collier Boulevard exit on I-75). In 2020, Phase I of the complex was completed and opened to the public. The facility is known as Paradise Coast Sports Complex and it is the mutha of all sports complexes. It covers 180 acres of land and will cost, when completed, about $100 million. Paradise Coast offers baseball, field hockey, football,

---

30   While Naples had one murder a year in 2019, Chicago had one every 18 hours.
31   As well as a few fun, but rather inactive sports, such as shuffleboard, mahjongg, canasta, and bocci.

lacrosse, rugby, running, soccer, an outdoor fitness center, a jogging trail, softball, ping-pong The National Sport of the People's Republic of China, (really!), and volleyball.

Paradise Coast also has a few non-sports amenities, including:

- An outdoor high-end concession

- A food market

- High-speed internet

- A thirty-two-acre lake (with beach)

- Five multipurpose artificial turf fields including a Championship Stadium that seats 3,500

(P.S. Phase II will add four new multipurpose fields.)

I first experienced the Paradise Coast Sports Complex when I drove NBA star Kenny Anderson to the complex. (See The NBA Player). He gave me a verbal tour and explained how the complex was bringing young athletes to Naples.

THE WACKY WORLD OF NAPLES

While Naples is a somewhat elderly and a rather wealthy community, it is certainly not staid (dull), stolid (emotionless), or boring (uninteresting). No, sir! In fact, Naples is the wackiest accumulation of prosperous old codgers on planet Earth. Here are a few examples of the area's abundant zaniness:

Tire Spikes aka Tire Destroyers

For some reason, a few communities in Naples ABSOLUTELY DO NOT WANT uninvited guests in their community. While firearms are common in Florida and are the best way to ward off would-be trespassers, these communities rely on a more down-to-earth method of preventing trespass—tire spikes. Tire spikes are designed to destroy all four tires of any car that improperly attempts to enter a community.

Unfancy Spikes at a Fancy Community

From a distance, these spikes look somewhat harmless, but beware, they're not!

Tire spikes are sharpened forged steel spikes anchored in the pavement that are optimally angled to puncture the tires of any car passing over them in the wrong direction. (No tire damage results from traveling in the correct direction.) Tire spikes are vicious-looking, especially up close and personal. Fortunately, their presence is always announced by one or more harshly worded signs.

Tire Spikes, up Close and Personal

Humorous (we hope) Signs

Naples' roads usually use the same traffic signs as the rest of the country. Occasionally, however, a few humorous, strange, non-governmental signs appear on Naples' highways, byways and parking lots. They are unique and I am pretty sure (but not positive) posted solely for their humor. In any case, they certainly provoke a smile.

The Name Game

A lot of places in the Naples area have very strange names. Here are a few examples.

Although it is in nearby Bonita Beach, this uniquely named bait and tackle shop sells T-shirts and hats that prominently display their name. In fact, they are one of the biggest T-shirt sellers in the area. Why? I don't know, perhaps their name has a ring to it! (Hint: Say it quickly!)

'Nuff said!

In addition to our sui generis bait and tackle shop, there are several other Naples emporia that sport unusual (but Hippielike) names.

2622
PEACE
LOVE
& LITTLE
DONUTS
HOURS
OPEN DAILY 7:00 - 2:00
(239) 213-0488

Twinkle Twinkle Little Store
Baby Gear Rental & Resale Boutique
OPEN

CHAPTER 4

Reality, Truths, and a Few Not-so-Fun Facts Vis-à-vis Naples

THE TIDE IS HIGH, BUT IT'S ALSO RED

The Gulf Coast of Southwest Florida is overflowing with beautiful beaches. Unfortunately, usually in the late summer or early fall, these beaches are also overflowing with blooms of Red Tide. Scientists have documented Red Ride blooms along Florida's Gulf Coast since the 1840s, and fish kills in Tampa Bay were mentioned in the logs of Spanish explorers.

Red Tide blooms are caused by the explosive growth of *karenia brevis*, a microscopic, single-celled algae. Blooms can last a month or more. Originally, it was thought that Red Tide was a naturally occurring phenomenon that originated offshore and moved toward the beaches. Recently, however, a University of Florida study found that "anthropogenic nitrogen runoff facilitated the growth of K. brevis blooms near Charlotte Harbor" and "bloom events would be mitigated by nitrogen source and transport controls within the Caloosahatchee and/or Kissimmee River basins."

My feelings exactly! Seriously though, I don't know what the University of Florida is talking about either, but I think they are hinting that human-generated pollution has something to do with Red Tide.

The funny thing about Red Tide is that it is rarely red. In fact, it usually has no color at all. The only indications of a Red Tide infestation are the dead fish littering the shoreline and the strong urge of bathers to cough when they approach the water.

A FEW BUMPS ALONG THE WAY

There are speed bumps almost everywhere in the world. But since Southwest Florida's climate is especially conducive to speed bump reproduction, they have multiplied wildly here. They have sprouted on the local streets, appeared in almost every parking lot, and grown on many through roads. There are so many speed bumps in the area that Naples is rapidly becoming the "Land of the Double Thump."

There are at least three species of speed bumps that are indigenous to Naples: the small speed bump, the medium speed bump, and the large speed bump.

Small speed bumps, also known as "strut busters," are the most irritating species of speed bump.[32] Thump . . . thump. They are usually two and one-half to three and one-half inches high and one to two feet in breadth. Thump . . . thump. If a small speed bump is traversed at a speed greater than 2.02 mph, they jar the car's suspension and rattle the driver's bones. Thump . . . thump. Worse, if a driver or a passenger is sitting in an awkward position, small speed bumps can be a real pain in the gonads. Thump . . . thump. (Author's

---

32   Guaranteed to destroy the struts (and shocks) of any car, foreign or domestic.

Note: when they are traversed, small speed bumps make a distinctive thump . . . thump sound.)

Medium speed bumps are easier to navigate than small ones. Thummmp . . . Thummmp. They are about the same height but are two to six feet in breadth, which allows them to be attacked at speeds of up to 25 mph without adverse effect to a car or its driver's body parts. Thummmp . . . Thummmp. For some strange reason, medium speed bumps are given strange names, like speed humps[33] or speed tables. (Author's Note: medium speed bumps produce a longer, less jarring, but still distinctive thummmp . . . thummmp sound.)

Large speed bumps are the most fun to navigate. They are over six feet in breadth and produce an entirely different sound when crossed. Whoosh . . . Whoosh. Large speed bumps can usually be crossed at speeds of 30 mph, but if their geometry is just right, they can be crossed at almost any speed (which makes you wonder what they are doing there in the first place). Spanning bumps with the "correct" geometry is like bobbing through an updraft in an airplane. Whoosh . . . Whoosh. The faster you go, the bigger you

---

33 C'mon, get your mind out of the gutter, literally.

bounce. (Author's Note: large speed bumps don't thump; they whoosh, distinctively!)

> **NOTES ON THE MEANING OF LIFE**—Fortunately, many speed bumps are installed on the cheap. This provides a driver with the opportunity to reduce automotive and anatomical damage. Inexpensively installed speed bumps do not extend from curb to curb. Instead, they barely span each lane of traffic (coming and going), leaving a small "speed bump gap" in the middle of the road. If a driver can navigate so that the left two wheels of the car roll through the gap, automotive and gonadal damage can be reduced by 50 percent!

FLORIDA DRIVERS—A STUDY IN DEPTH

Floridians are the most tolerant and friendly people in the world, until they get into a car. Then, all bets are off. Once ensconced in an automobile, Floridians become slow,[34] hyper-cautious, and anything but friendly. They drive below the speed limit, they take forever to make a driving decision, and they honk a lot.

When a Floridian driver approach a stop sign, not only do they come to a full stop at every sign, but they also give the sign a standing eight count before continuing down the road. Florida drivers honk their horn at almost everything: other drivers who don't immediately start moving when a light turns green; other drivers who cut in front of them,

---

34 Since I always "observe what I see," I noticed the slowest Florida drivers are also the shortest in stature. I don't know why.

regardless of the space between the cars; and crossing drivers who stop past a stop line.

> **NOTES ON THE MEANING OF LIFE**—Many Florida drivers execute what I call "The Delayed Honk." When another driver does something untoward to a "delayed honker", the "delayed honker" doesn't honk right away, only when he or the offending driver turn onto another street. Since this could be two or three minutes later, the offending driver is usually left more confused than chastened.

The hyper-cautiousness displayed by Florida drivers when driving is nothing to the hyper-cautiousness they display when they're turning. A Florida driver won't attempt a right turn if there is anything, and I mean anything (automobile, airplane, train, bicycle, tricycle, barge, unicycle, trolley, moped, motorcycle, tram, scooter, boat, bus, autogiro, spacecraft, rickshaw, monorail, sedan chair, blimp, dirigible, zeppelin, or helicopter) on the left horizon, as far as the eye can see! Worse, if a Florida driver is making a *left* turn, all three horizons (left, right, and straight ahead) must be 100 percent clear (as far as the eye can see) before the turn will be attempted.

Thanks to their hyper-cautiousness, many Florida drivers traditionally drive 4–9 mph below the posted speed limit (except on interstates, where they drive at the appropriate —80–90 mph—speed). Thus, when a Florida driver is driving ahead of a "normal" driver on a single-lane roadway, that driver becomes a Mobile Obstacle (aka MO). An MO will force all following drivers to limp along behind them, sometimes for hours, traveling at the MO's usual speed (4-9 mph below the posted limit). Additionally, an MO will often, recklessly and out of nowhere, "squirt" on to a one-lane road, in front of a "normal" driver or drivers, and immediately begin "blocking the herd" by driving at their usual snail's pace (4-9 mph below the posted limit). MOs only increase their speed (uncharacteristically rapidly) when a following driver moves into the oncoming lane in an attempt to pass the MO.

MOs can also clog multi-lane roadways. But to do so, they must team up with one of more accomplices to form a Florida Flying Pick. And, to add insult to insult, the most sophisticated Flying Florida Picks employ Delta-V Management.

What is Flying Florida Pick with Delta-V Management? There are two parts to the answer. A pick is a tactic in sports whereby one or more players slow down or stop on the court or field to prevent opposing players from getting past them. A Flying Florida Pick is the same thing, except it is executed on multi-lane highways by MOs in motion. To form a Flying Florida Pick, two or MOs motor along, side-by-side, one car per lane, at the same slow speed (at *exactly the same slow speed*). This prevents "opposing" drivers following them from ever passing the "Pick".

Drivers participating in a "Pick" can also employ Delta-V Management to further aggravate the slowdown. Delta-V is a scientific term that means change in velocity (i.e., how quickly something accelerates—speeds up—or decelerates — slows down). MOs in a "Pick" utilize Delta-V Management by speeding up or slowing down (for a stop sign or light) *simultaneously and at the exact same rate of acceleration or deceleration* (i.e., they manage their Delta-V). This prevents "opposing" drivers following a "Pick" from passing even when the "Pick" is changing speed.

RED LIGHT GREEN LIGHT

In addition to having slow drivers, Florida has the slowest traffic lights in the Western Hemisphere. They take forever to turn green. While driving for Uber, I spent a lot of time waiting at lights and had a chance to observe them, up close and personal. I discovered the traffic lights in Naples are normally green for forward-moving traffic only 25 percent of the time. The rest of the light's green time, so to speak, is spent elsewhere: 25 percent of it permitting cross traffic to go straight ahead; 25 percent of it permitting cross traffic to turn left; and 25 percent of it permitting forward-moving and oncoming traffic to turn left. (These ratios can vary depending on location and time of day.)

Yellow lights also create a problem here. In most of the known universe, it is legal and common (very common) for drivers, if oncoming traffic permits, to turn left when a traffic light is yellow. Not in Florida. Here, drivers who are planning to turn left stop dead at every yellow light, regardless of whether there is oncoming traffic or not. They only turn left on a green light or a green arrow!

Naples' drivers' aversion to turning left on yellow, along with the area's slow traffic lights, cause delays that are overwhelming. The roads are so slow that I began crocheting while waiting at red traffic lights! (Editor's Note: No, he didn't!)

CHAPTER 5

Passengers—The Good, the Bad, and the Ugly!

ALL THE EVIL UNDER THE SUN

All my passengers, with two exceptions, were wonderful, or at least somewhat sane. This passenger was the first exception. I was called to pick her up on a bright, summer morning, around 11:30 a.m. I quickly noticed that there were a few unusual aspects to this call. First, the Uber driver's app didn't provide me with the destination, only a cryptic note saying the passenger would supply the destination address. Then, on my way to the passenger's house, the app alerted me to be very careful because the passenger was very old.

When I arrived, I saw that the alert was correct. The passenger and her husband were each on the far side of eighty. Through a heavy German accent, the woman explained to me that the ride was ordered through an elder care service company that helps the elderly in their day-to-day living (and sends notes to Uber drivers warning them to be careful because their customers are old). Then she told me we would be going to an animal hospital where she had an appointment for her little dog. Things began to get strange when the woman said that neither she nor her husband knew the hospital's name or location.

"The service company told us you would know how to get to the animal hospital," she announced.

"I wasn't given the name or address of the hospital. Are you sure you don't have it?" I replied.

"No, they said you would know it."

Hmm, I thought, *this is going to get interesting*.

"Do you have the name or address written down anywhere?" I asked.

Both the passenger and her husband shuffled some papers and replied, "No," almost in unison.

After a rather uncomfortable pause, I called the service company and they gave me the information. I entered the address into my GPS and we were on our way. The drive would take about ten minutes.

As soon as we began our trip, things got stranger. The passenger complained Red Flame was too hot, so I turned up the air conditioning. Then she complained it was too cold, so I turned the A/C back down. Then she complained the car was "too dark." It does have a black interior, but it was a bright sunny day! To appease the lady, I turned on the dome light. Best I could do!

Then the strangeness turned into evil. My passenger began to criticize me personally and, just as we arrived at the animal hospital, she, out of the blue, called me a racist. (No, I never called her a Nazi.) I didn't reply because a) I didn't know what to say; and b) I assumed the woman would be quickly exiting my car. Spoiler alert: No such luck!

This ride occurred during the Covid pandemic, when

animal hospitals would not allow any man, woman, or beast into their facility until the time of their appointment. Here's the rub: the woman had misread her appointment time and we were two hours early. Of course, she blamed me for the error.

I offered to drive the passenger and her dog back to their house, but she (the passenger, not the dog) refused and ordered me to wait in the car with her (and her dog) until their appointment. I was surprised she wanted to wait two hours in a hot/cold/dark/dome light-lit car, with a racist Uber driver, but she was insistent on it. Of course, I told her I couldn't wait.

"Well, in that case, I am not getting out of the car," she threatened.

To be honest, for a minute or so, I didn't know what to do. Then, I decided to call the police.

"If you don't leave the car, I am going to have to call the police," I told her.

"If you do, I am going to have my lawyer call you right away."

With some justification, I got a little flippant. "Not a problem," I replied. "I was a lawyer for thirty-five years. Maybe we could talk shop."

She didn't respond to me, nor did she call her lawyer. But she didn't leave, so I called the cops.

Shortly, a sheriff's deputy arrived. Per police procedure, took me aside and got my side of the story. Then he walked over and talked to the passenger, who immediately raised her voice and began loudly criticizing both me and the deputy, in two languages.

Eventually, the deputy convinced the passenger (and her

dog[35]) to leave the car. Then he walked over to my side of the car and asked me if I was paid in full. Since payment comes directly from Uber and I didn't expect a tip, I said, "Yes."

He leaned into my window and said quietly, "You can escape now."

I never got a call from the lady's attorney, but she did file a complaint with Uber, alleging I was unreasonable. I talked to Uber and they told me not to worry about it.

THERE ARE A MILLION STORIES IN THE NAKED CITY. THIS IS THE BEST!

There are two Ritz Hotels in Naples. The slightly fancier one is on the beach and is known as the beach resort, while the slightly less fancy (but still damn fancy) Ritz is inland, has a golf course, and is known as the golf resort.

On December 10, the golf resort hosted the Live Fest Concert. This concert was extremely popular and I drove many passengers there that afternoon.

On one trip, my passengers were two women in their mid-thirties. One was tall, thin, and model-like, while the other was more Playmatish. Both were very pretty. I picked them up in Bonita Beach for the fifteen-minute ride to the concert venue.

My passengers and I chatted briefly. Then, they began to talk among themselves. Although I couldn't hear the entire conversation, they were intently discussing sexuality, sexual

---

35   I was tempted to call him a dirty, mangy mutt, but he was really a friendly, well groomed, and cute terrier.

activity, body part size, and B&D[36].

Just when I thought the ride couldn't get any more… well, you know, the Playmatish woman noticed that her very skimpy sundress was inside-out. She asked me if it would be all right if she took it off, turned it right side out, and put it back on. All while seated in the back seat of my car!

Talk about no brainers!

"Sure," I replied. "Since I'm a gentleman; I won't look."

"Oh, don't worry about it," purred Miss December, "You can look all you want!"

Since I always comply with every passenger request, I did.

My mother always told me to try to learn something new every day. On that December day, I learned that there are women in Naples whose sole articles of attire are a skimpy sundress and two sandals.

THE FORMER NFL QUARTERBACK

One of my passengers was a former NFL quarterback. He had played for several teams in the '60s and '70s. He regaled me with tales of his life in professional football and said Don Shula was the smartest coach he ever met.

THE MAN WHO KNEW MR. DIVOSTA

One morning, I picked up an elderly Hispanic man. We got to talking about the past and present real estate development in Naples. He told me that before he retired, he had been a ceramic tile installer and had worked in Naples for many years. When I mentioned I used to live in Verona Walk, the

---

36   Bondage and discipline. Not to be confused with D&B (Dun & Bradstreet).

passenger informed me (although I already knew) that all the communities in and near Naples with "Walk" in their name were built by DiVosta Home Builders. He said he worked for DiVosta for most of his career and he had gotten to know Mr. DiVosta (that would be Otto "Buz" DiVosta) personally. The passenger added that Mr. DiVosta was the nicest man as well as the best builder in all of Florida. I never met Mr. DiVosta, but I can attest to the fact he builds quality homes!

> **NOTES ON THE MEANING OF LIFE**—DiVosta also developed a quick-setting cement and could build a three-bedroom, two-bath home, with a two-car garage, in seven hours and thirty-five minutes!

THE REALLY, REALLY, OLD (BUT REALLY, REALLY, SPRY) LADY

Without a doubt, the oldest person who ever told me a story of the Naples of long ago was a woman in her nineties. She told me that she grew up in Naples during the 1940s and that right after WWII, her father opened a combination general store, liquor store, and bar at Fifth Avenue South and Tamiami Trail, which, today, is smack dab in the heart of (Fifth Avenue) downtown Naples. She further mentioned that even though her house was on Third Avenue South (two blocks north) and Sixth Street (another three blocks west), the general store/liquor store/bar was visible from her home. She said her mother liked the fact she could always tell when her husband was on his way home. Today, several tall buildings and a multi-story parking garage obstruct that view.

For some reason (probably maybe because I'm a fan of old bars), I discussed the general store/liquor store/bar combo with other, mostly elderly, passengers. They told me that the bar was called the Eagle's Nest and the complex was actually located on Tamiami Trail, a block north Fifth Avenue South

All the passengers spoke highly of the Eagle's Nest (apparently, they were fans of old bars, too). A few told me that when Florida prohibited the sale of alcohol after 3 a.m., the law had a "grandfather" clause that allowed bars that had been staying open all night to continue to do so. They added that when the Eagle's Nest finally closed (somewhere around 1975), it was the last all-night bar in Naples.

NORTHERN IMMIGRATION—THE OLD-FASHIONED WAY

I heard an interesting story one morning while I was driving a really senior couple to the airport. The elderly gent began talking about life in old Naples. He said his grandfather came to Naples in 1920 and started a construction business that has been run by the passenger's family ever since.

I was more than a little surprised when the passenger explained how difficult it was to get to Naples in those days. In 1920, the only way to enter Naples was to take the train to Punta Gorda (which is about sixty-five miles north of Naples) and then board a boat for a six-hour voyage to The Naples Pier.

I researched the matter and found that the first road into Naples, which originated in Fort Myers, was completed in 1921, while rail service to Naples was not inaugurated until The Orange Blossom Special arrived in 1927. Before that, anyone wanting to enter Naples had to take the train to the boat to the pier.

THE WINE AND BEER GIRL FROM CRAYTON ROAD

One of the strangest experiences I had as an Uber driver occurred shortly after I began driving. Late one evening, I got a call to a house on Crayton Road, an upscale neighborhood in the City of Naples. As soon as I stopped in the driveway, a rather pretty, but somewhat disheveled young woman, walked to my car and said, "Hi, I don't really need a ride anywhere, but I will pay you $100 if you get me some wine, beer, and potato chips."[37]

Knowing a good thing when I heard one, I quickly asked, "Any particular brand of chips?"

"No," she said, "And I don't care what kind of wine you get either. Just spend about $20 a bottle."

I drove to the nearest 7-Eleven, bought the merchandise, brought it back to Crayton Road, and collected my professional shopper's fee.

THE LONG AND WINDING ROAD

Many passengers have asked me, "What was your longest ride?" The answer to this question depends upon whether you consider distance or duration.

The prize for my longest distance ride was a trip of 140 miles. My passenger was a charter airline pilot who had just dropped off "his" plane at Naples Airport. I was tasked with taking him home to South Miami. Although the trip was

---

37   This was before Uber began offering a food shopping service.

long, distance wise, it only took an hour and fifty minutes. The reason for the "short" duration of the trip was that most of the journey was on I-75 (aka Alligator Alley), a two-lane highway that spans the breadth of Florida. Everyone speeds on Alligator Alley.

Even though the trip took a while, time seemed to fly by because both the pilot and I were avid conversationalists. We both liked talking about the things that interested us and we were both interested in the same things (mainly cars and aviation, but also women). We had an interesting and extended conversation for the entire trip.

The longest duration single stop I ever took lasted over two hours. The trip began while I was waiting in the Uber lot at RSW Airport. I got a call to pick up Kathy at the Arrivals terminal. Kathy turned out to be a very pretty, very young (about twenty-one) woman who was traveling to a friend's parents' condominium in Sarasota, about ninety-five miles away. Kathy was a college student so, during the trip, we discussed the differences between colleges today and colleges when I was a student (back in the late Renaissance). We concluded that, apart from still having to listen to boring teachers and having difficulties scheduling classes, college life today is very different than when I was a struggling student. Kathy seemed surprised when I told her that when I was a student, we had to use steam-powered computers. (I don't think she believed me.)

The duration of the above trips paled in comparison to my longest multi-stop journey. One morning, as I was out trolling the streets of Laredo[38], er, of Naples, I was called to pick up a passenger from a community off Immokalee Road.

38 *Streets of Laredo*, a great cowboy song by Marty Robbins.

When I arrived at the pickup, the passenger, his wife, and his daughter got into the car. My passenger was from the islands (the Caribbean, not Staten, Manhattan, or Long) and was very friendly, although he seemed a little stressed.

Our first leg of the trip was to Fort Myers. After a forty-minute drive we arrived at a large building. I parked and the passenger got out of the car. He told me he had to pick up some papers and would be back in ten minutes or so. His family also left the car to take a short walk around downtown Fort Myers. After everyone left the car, I noticed I was parked next to the Fort Myers U.S. Courthouse & Federal Building.

After about twenty minutes, my passenger and his family seemed to materialize simultaneously. The all got into the car. I noticed that the passenger looked even more stressed.

After a short ride across town, we arrived at our next stop, a plain-looking office building. As we stopped, I asked my if there was a men's room in the building and, if so, did he think I could use it. He said "of course" and guided me to the third floor. As soon as we left the elevator, I saw that we had entered the U.S. Federal Public Defender's Office. Security was strict. When I asked to use the men's room, I had to be escorted to the men's room by a female U.S. marshal (She waited outside). As I left the office a few minutes later, I saw the passenger still in the waiting room; he really looked stressed to the max!

After we were all back in the car, we headed towards our next destination, a school bus stop back in Naples. When we arrived there, we waited for the passenger's son's school bus.

As soon as his son (who looked to be about eight years

old) left the bus, the passenger picked him up and carried him son back to the car. For the first time that day, I saw the passenger smile; his stress seemed to have disappeared.

Finally, our last stop was back to the family's house. On the way there, the passenger was playing with his son and didn't seem to have a care in the world. After the ride, when the passenger thanked me for the ride, he had a big smile on his face. The family and I had spent almost three hours together; we felt like the best of friends.

A SHORT HOP?

One morning, just before Christmas, I was driving past the Coastland Mall (the mall that was to be burned down by protestors) and got a call for a one-minute trip. I had never been offered such a short trip, so I accepted the call to see who needed an Uber ride for only one minute.

The pickup was at the main entrance to Macy's Department Store. When I arrived, I saw an incredibly old and very disheveled gentleman in a walker waiting next to an almost as old lady who was dressed as one of Santa's elves.

It turned out that the old guy was my passenger and the elf was a Macy's employee, dressed for the holidays.

After I stopped at the entrance, Ms. Elf and I started to help the old gent transfer from his walker to the car. Suddenly, he took a terrible fall. Somehow, as he was slowly moving the last foot or so to the car, he misstepped, flew up in the air, and came down with a crash. His fall opened numerous bloody scratches on the passenger's leg and caused his pants to come down to his knees.

With much difficulty, Ms. Elf and I righted the passenger

and pulled up his pants. She quickly went inside to get some paper towels and bandages, leaving me alone with my bleeding and agitated future rider. I tried to calm him down, but he appeared to have dementia and didn't want to be calmed. Then, all of a sudden, he became quiet.

Ms. Elf returned with the towels and bandages and we cleaned up the passenger's leg as best we could. After I thanked Ms. Elf, the passenger and I got started the trip. Following the directions of my Uber Driver's app, I drove to the far end of Macy's parking lot and my app intoned, "You have arrived."

"Is this where you want to go?" I asked the passenger.

"No, I have to go to North Naples."

Considering the passenger's mental state, I decided to avoid excessive conversation and merely asked, "What address in North Naples?"

The passenger gave me the address and added, "I don't know how to use the Uber thing on my phone. Could you help? The elf lady put in the trip."

The passenger handed me his phone. As I was entering the trip, he instructed, "Put in a $5 tip for yourself."

Since I always try to comply with every passenger request, I did as instructed. We drove to the destination, which turned out to be a retirement home.

Before I could help the passenger from the car, he again took out his phone and exclaimed, "I am going to give you a $5 tip."

"I already gave myself a $5 tip, like you asked," I altruistically responded.

"No, you didn't," he replied, his dementia returning as he

appeared to enter another tip.

Finally, I was able to help the passenger from the car and into the facility. As I drove away, I saw that I received a $5.05 tip. Apparently, my passenger attempted to add a second $5 tip, but misplaced the decimal point.

P.S. The "one-minute" trip took fifty-eight minutes.

JACK THE SCRATCHER

My ride with Jack was a short one. We didn't talk much because he spent the whole ride scratching what seemed to be every part of his body. When he did mention he played golf, I was tempted to ask if he was a scratch golfer[39] but didn't. As a precaution, after Jack's trip, I had Red Flame deloused. (Editor's Note: No, he didn't.)

MY BUDDY FROM BIRTH

I was talking to a passenger one afternoon and he mentioned he was born in Newark Presbyterian Hospital. Lo and behold, I was born at the same hospital!

"You weren't there around March 19, 1953, were you." I asked.

"Yes," he exclaimed. "I was born on March 20th."

Unfortunately, neither the passenger nor I remembered each other even though we were in the same nursery.

NOTES ON THE MEANING OF LIFE—Whitney Houston

39   "Scratch golfer" means that the golfer being referred to has a handicap of 0 or below. i.e., an incredibly good golfer.

was also born at Newark Presbyterian, but neither of us remembered meeting her either.

THREE CHICKS FROM CHICAGO, BOATUS RIDEUM, AND CRIME

One morning, I picked up three women in North Naples. The women were from Chicago and were headed to Tin City to embark on a sunset cruise. They didn't know what to call their trip. I told them that when I was in law school, my school's annual boat trip around Manhattan Island was called Boatus Rideum. My passengers liked the name.

During the drive, I asked the ladies what they liked the most about Naples.

"Well," they replied, "last night, WINK News reported the only crime committed in Naples was the theft of a golf cart. Crime reports in Chicago are a bit longer."

They quickly added, "And we don't think defunding the police will help the problem."

We all laughed.

THE SEARCH FOR GREEN ENERGY

The background: Like most former hippies, I love "green" energy, especially when it doesn't cost me anything or cause me any inconvenience. When I moved to Naples, I discovered that a plethora of, now elderly and single, hippie chicks also lived here. Presumably, they, like me, also love "green" energy, especially when it comes in an expensive car attached to a rich guy. Thus, when a wealthy man from Naples buys an expensive, showy, but "green" car he is "in like sin" with the town's elderly hippie chicks.

The story: One afternoon, I picked up a passenger who was going to Fort Myers.

He told me he was interested in sports cars and complimented me on Red Flame (he especially liked the color). He said Audis were his second favorite sports car.

"What's your favorite sports car?" I asked.

"We're going to pick it up now," he replied. "A Tesla."

I was impressed. One of my friends had a Tesla and the car fascinated me.

During the half-hour drive, my passenger and I discussed Audis, Teslas, and, occasionally, women. He told me that since there were no Tesla dealers in Naples, he had to go to Fort Myers to have the car serviced.

"You mean if a wealthy guy from Naples buys an incredibly expensive, green energy car to impress elderly hippie chicks, he has to travel all the way from wealthy Naples to moderately incomed Fort Myers to buy it and have it serviced?" I asked incredulously. "What in God's name is a monied Neapolitan male to do?"

"Don't worry," my passenger replied, "a Tesla dealership is opening in Naples soon."

As we arrived at the dealership, I asked the passenger how he liked his Tesla.

The climax: "Well," he replied with a wink, "since I got it, I've become a lot better looking and all my jokes are now funny!"

> **NOTES ON THE MEANING OF LIFE**—Money can't buy love, but it sure improves your bargaining position!

(Author's Plea: Elon, Naples is awash in money and in well-heeled men who need a "green" car to impress the hippie chicks who ignored them in high school. Please open the Tesla dealership here quickly! The landed [and corporate securitied] gentry of Naples need you!)

THE LORD (RET.) OF LORDSTOWN

One afternoon, I was called to a small waterside park across the inlet from Tin City. When I arrived, an elderly couple was awaiting me. When they got into the car, they told me one of the pontoons of their party boat sprang a leak, which, in nautical terms, caused a 40^0 list. (In non-nautical terms, the boat was sinking.) Fortunately, they were able to save the boat by beaching it at the park.

We started driving towards their house to get help for the boat. During the drive, the male passenger mentioned he used to be the mayor of Lordstown, Ohio. He seemed to be a little laid back (as did his wife) for a politician, but when he began talking, I saw he knew his stuff. I told him the only thing I knew about Lordstown was that GM closed a plant there several years ago.

"Yes, GM broke their word to me and to the town," he replied. "They said they would keep the plant open until 2028, but they didn't."

"What did you do?" I asked.

"Well, there wasn't much I could do about the car plant, but I did convince them to open a battery plant in town. I also arranged for Home Goods to open a large distribution center in Lordstown."

The mayor seemed sincerely interested in the welfare of Lordstown and its residents. I was so engrossed in our conversation, I forgot to ask the mayor if he was a Republican or a Democrat.

THE IMPERIOUS TEACHER

Early one morning, the day after Election Day 2020 (and still during the Covid pandemic), I picked up a passenger in a semi-upscale neighborhood of Naples off Goodlette-Frank Road. She got into the car, quickly identified herself as a teacher, and just as quickly (and before I could don my mask) forcefully queried, "Sir, will you be masked?"

"Absolutely," I said. *Hi-Ho Silver* went unsaid.

> **NOTES ON THE MEANING OF LIFE**—Silver was the mount of The Lone Ranger, who was always masked.

During the drive, she told me that, since Biden had now been elected, our country was on the road to redemption. I kept my own counsel.

THE NBA PLAYER

In addition to driving a former NFL quarterback, I also drove a former National Basketball Association star. I got a call to pick up a Kenny at the Parrot Bar and Grill (the one in Naples, not the one in Casablanca).

> **NOTES ON THE MEANING OF LIFE**—The Blue Parrot was the "other" bar in the 1942 movie *Casablanca*, a film that portrayed the world's greatest love story.[40]

When I got there, an athletic and robust-looking middle-aged man got into the car. During our twenty-minute drive, he explained he was visiting Naples to run a basketball camp for kids. Slowly, the passenger began to look familiar. When I asked him if he had ever played professional sports, he told me he was former NBA player Kenny Anderson. We had an enjoyable conversation. In fact, it turned out Kenny and I are landsmen; he was from Queens, while I was from adjacent Nassau County. He also went to Archbishop Malloy High School with a friend of mine. Kenny is now the head men's basketball coach at Fisk University. He told me to look him up any time I am in Nashville. (Author's Note: When I told Kenny that I was writing a book, he insisted I use his real name.)

> **NOTES ON THE MEANING OF LIFE**—Landsman comes from Yiddish. It means a person who comes from the same area or town.

EAST OF EDEN—THE WILD, WILD EAST OF EDEN

The largest (by far) and the wildest (also by far) area in Naples is Golden Gate Estates (not to be confused with

---

40   Which, strangely, contained almost no romance!

Golden Gate City, which is much smaller and much more civilized). Golden Gate Estates is a huge tract of land to which the rule of law and power of electricity have only recently arrived.

On the 5th of July, I picked up a thirties-something fellow from what looked like a homestead deep in Golden Gate Estates. During the ride, I asked him if he had an enjoyable 4th.

"We sure did," he replied. "Everyone on my street (of approximately twenty to thirty houses) came outside after dinner. We kept firing our guns and setting off fireworks until the sun went down. Then we drank our heads off until almost midnight."

It may be impolitic to say so, but I wish I was there!

HEY, MR. SPICE MAN (FROM BALTIMORE)

One afternoon, I drove an interesting fellow from Baltimore named Miles. We quickly started discussing the economy and business environment of Maryland in general and Baltimore. In particular.

According to the Economic Profile prepared by the Baltimore Development Corporation, the city's main industries are financial & professional services, health & bioscience technology, culture & tourism, information & creative services, logistics, and advanced manufacturing.

Of course, the Development Corporation doesn't know what they're talking about. Both Miles and I agreed that Baltimore has had, and continues to have, only one industry of note: the production and distribution of Old Bay Seasoning.

For those of you who don't live either within a one-hundred-mile radius of Baltimore or in the rural South, Old Bay Seasoning is a spice used by locals on almost anything. It tastes like a little bit of everything because it contains a little bit of everything, celery salt, black pepper, crushed red pepper flakes, paprika, laurel leaves, mustard, salt, cardamom, cloves, and ginger.

Baltimoreans love Old Bay Seasoning. One of my friends is from Baltimore and he uses so much of it that he buys it in fifty-pound boxes.[41] He puts Old Bay on just about everything except breakfast food and desserts.

I told Miles this story and he topped it! He said his brother even puts Old Bay on corn flakes and ice cream!

Just before Miles left the car, I asked him how the new mayor of Baltimore working out. Miles said was happy with new mayor, who he said was slightly less corrupt than the previous four.

RIP-OFF RAQUEL

Rip-off Raquel was another passenger (actually, she was only a potential passenger) who wasn't very decent or very nice, at least not to me. I thought you might find it interesting to see how even a friendly, resourceful, and highly efficient Uber driver can get screwed, blued, and tattooed by an indecent, not-so-nice, potential passenger.

To understand this story, you must be aware of several to an Uber driver's compensation. Three applied to Raquel's request for a ride.

---

41   Available online for $297.54.

1. If a pickup is expected to, and, in fact, takes longer than eleven minutes, the driver is entitled to a Pickup Premium; and

2. If a drive has to wait more than three minutes for a passenger to get into the car, the driver is entitled to a waiting charge; and

3. Finally, if a ride is cancelled more than five minutes after it was ordered, the driver is entitled to a cancelation fee.

Inexplicably, Raquel found a way to cancel a trip that had accrued a Pickup Premium, a waiting charge, _and_ a cancellation fee and pay nothing!

Here's how that scoundrel did it. The pickup time was scheduled for twenty-two minutes and, in fact, it took me twenty-three minutes for me to reach the gate at Lely Resort (Raquel's community). Hence, a Pickup Premium was due.

As soon as I arrived at the gate, I called Raquel for the gate code so I could gain entrance. enter the community. She told me to wait at the gate and she would walk to my car. (I often get this request at gated communities.)

I waited at the gate for six minutes. Since this was over three minutes, this ride qualified for a waiting charge.

I called Raquel again. She didn't answer and sent a text canceling the trip. Since the trip was cancelled more than five minutes after it was ordered, I was entitled to a cancellation charge.

I had driven for twenty-three minutes, waited for six minutes, and the trip was ultimately canceled, so I expected to be paid a $5 Pickup Premium, a $2 waiting charge, and a $3.60 cancelation fee. However, as soon as Raquel cancelled, my Uber driver app showed I would receive nothing!

WTF? How did a wealthy Lely resident defraud such a friendly, resourceful, and highly efficient Uber driver? I called Uber to find out. They told me that when a driver exceeds the estimated pickup time by more than five minutes, the passenger can cancel the trip at any time and pay nothing. I did not know that. They also told me when a passenger pays nothing, the driver receives nothing. I knew that.

Since Raquel kept me waiting at the gate, I never reached her house, so my time spent waiting (six minutes) was not considered waiting time but was added to the twenty-three-minute pickup time. This generated an actual pickup time of twenty-nine minutes, which was greater than the twenty-seven minutes (scheduled pickup time of twenty-two minutes plus five minutes grace) permitted. This allowed Raquel to cancel the ride and pay nothing! allowed. Boy, was I steamed!

In Raquel's defense, I must say that when I talked to her on the phone, she didn't seem to be the sharpest knife in the drawer. So, her heinous and notorious "fraud" might be due more to obliviousness than to malice. After all, she still had to call (and pay for) another Uber.

Of course, I was really irate at being "defrauded" by Raquel (after all, an extra $10.60 can always come in handy). I thought of starting a class war against the wealthy in Lely Resort by spray painting "Attica, Attica, Attica" everywhere I could, but I didn't. Instead, I just bitched and moaned to Uber and they gave me the $3.60 cancelation fee.

> **NOTES ON THE MEANING OF LIFE**—The 1971 prisoners at the Attica (New York) Correctional Facility fomented a rebellion (a class war of sorts) that resulted in the loss of forty-three lives.

AULD LANG SYNE

At the stroke of midnight 2021/22, I was in Red Flame, driving a passenger with the strange name of Matthewluke and his wife to the Mercato. I didn't kiss either of them, but we each downed a few bottles of Dom Perignon to ring in the New Year! (Editor's Note: No, they didn't!)

THE IMMOKALEE ROAD ENGINEER

Three-lane Immokalee Road is one of the slowest east-west arteries in all of Naples, especially after the snowbirds arrive for the winter.

One day, as I was driving an elderly passenger along the crowded road, I commented on the heavy traffic. The passenger told me he was a retired traffic engineer and, as a retirement project, he had analyzed the traffic on Immokalee Road. He concluded that over 80 percent of the time, the center lane is the fastest lane of travel. During my subsequent travels on Immokalee Road, I kept an eye on the traffic and the engineer was right; the center lane was usually the fastest moving lane. (Author's Note to snowbirds only: I am lying. When on Immokalee Road, always drive in the left or right lane; never drive in the center lane.) (Editor's Note: No, he's not lying!)

JASONKIDD

On numerous occasions, I was called to drive a rather friendly African American teenager whose Uber app name was Jasonkidd (no space). Since he only appeared to be eighteen, or so, and didn't seem tall enough to play in the NBA, I think he was using an alias.

AN OLD PASSENGER, MR. JONDAHL, AND WAYZATA, MINNESOTA

One afternoon, I picked up a passenger who turned out to be a lot older than he looked. During the drive, he told me he spent his career in the insurance business in Minnesota. I mentioned my father was also in the insurance business and in 1968 (fifty-two years prior), our family traveled to Minnesota and visited one of my father's business associates, who was also an insurance man.

"What was the executive's name?" the passenger asked, "I might know him."

Fat chance, I thought, but I replied (and was amazed I remembered the name), "Don Jondahl."

Oh, I know Don," the passenger exclaimed. "You must have stayed at his farm in Wayzata!"

Incredible, I thought. A human connection after fifty-two years of time and 1,721 miles of distance. Words failed me.

TALKATIVE TED

I was called to pick up a passenger near Fifth Avenue South in downtown Naples and take him to Cape Coral, about an hour's drive away. As soon as I picked up Ted, he started talking about everything under the sun, including his love life, about which he was providing too much information! I couldn't get a word in edgewise, so after ten minutes or so, I stopped trying. For the last fifty minutes of the trip, Ted rambled on, not even noticing I wasn't taking part in the "dialogue." As I dropped Ted off, I suggested he get a job as a "talking head" on a TV news program.

THE ~~GUN NUT~~ SECOND AMENDMENT ADVOCATE

In the middle of the summer, I picked up a thirties-something male on Immokalee Road and drove him to a Mexican restaurant three miles away. As soon as the passenger got into the car, he asked me, "You got any guns?"

"No," I responded.

"You must be new to Florida," he countered. "Everyone needs a few guns down here."

"Well," I offered, not wanting to begin a serious constitutional argument on a four-minute trip, "they are expensive. I'd rather not spend the money."

My remarks provoked an immediate retort from the passenger on how to save money on the purchase of firearms and how to profit from transactions in them.

"You look like someone who needs a 40 cal. Smith & Wesson semi-automatic pistol. It holds fifteen rounds and there is a shop in Bonita Springs selling them for $399 during their Labor Day sale, which is only a few weeks away." He continued, "You can also pick up an AR-15 rifle at the same shop. They sell the parts for less than $350. If you smuggle it into Mexico and put it together, you can sell it for over $5,000! That's a lot of money!"

Fortunately, we arrived at the Mexican restaurant just before our discussion became illegally conspiratorial. My passenger said goodbye, gave me the thumbs-up, and hopped out of the car.

In a way, I was fortunate. I thought, *you never know. If Uber doesn't work out, at least I have a new career path to pursue!*

NAPLES' FIRST ITALIAN, FIRST PIZZA, AND FIRST AIRSTRIP

One of my most interesting passengers, historically speaking, was a young man I drove home. He lived four blocks east of Tamiami Trail a little north of where the Bascom Palmer Eye Center sits today.

He explained he lived in the house his grandfather had built when he came to Naples in the early 1930s. Not only was his grandfather one of the first Italians to settle in Naples (Did you notice how all the other founders of Naples were WASPs? Well, at least they had WASPy names.), he also opened the first Italian restaurant in Naples (four blocks away on Tamiami Trail) and built the first airstrip in town (which ran from his restaurant to his house).

The restaurant served pizza, which was also probably a first for Naples since pizza wasn't widely sold in America until the 1950s.

> **NOTES ON THE MEANING OF LIFE**—Prior to World War II, pizza was also known as tomato pie.

Since I am a fan of Italians, pizza, and airplanes, I enjoyed talking to my Italo-American connazionale. Che bello!

THE MOORING LINE DRIVE MAVEN

Mooring Line Drive is a pretty street in a pretty upscale neighborhood of Naples. It is an older street that was originally lined with small 1960s ranch-type houses. However, only a few of these houses remain; the rest were bought by the rich and bulldozed to make way for new McMansions. (A little economic envy humor on my part. In fact, the new houses on Mooring Line Drive are very big and very nice.) The result is that today, Mooring Line Drive is an eclectic collection of big, small, new, and old houses.

> **NOTES ON THE MEANING OF LIFE**—According to 2020 real estate records, the value of the homes on Mooring Line Drive ranges from $210,000 to $5,000,000.

One afternoon, I drove a passenger to Mooring Line Drive and dropped him off at a modest, but nice house. During the drive, he had volunteered the name, background, and economic status of almost every resident of the street. He said the residents of Mooring Line Drive included expatriates from five countries and a descendent of Barron Collier. He also told me he was friendly with everyone on the street! I hope that his "friends" are still his friends after they read this book!

SARAH FROM SOUTH AFRICA

I picked up a passenger in Golden Gate City whose name was Sarah. She came from South Africa and had the best English accent I ever heard. We didn't have much in common, but I kept the conversation up just so I could listen to her euphonious voice.

ALL THINGS BRIGHT AND BEAUTIFUL

One afternoon, I was called for a ride by a Jewish, Ukrainian woman from New York City named Sandy. I drove her somewhere, but I don't remember where. The reason I don't remember where is that my mind was on something else. What was the something else? Well, my passenger was the most beautiful woman I have ever seen (partially because she looked Italian). Sandy and I talked for most of the ride, but I can't remember much of what we talked about either.

For some reason (probably my real-world experience), I expected such a beautiful woman to be stuck up; she wasn't. To be unfriendly; she wasn't. To be dumb; she wasn't. And to be selfish; she wasn't. In fact, she was the prettiest, nicest, most intelligent, friendliest, and most family-oriented woman (she also had the hottest body) in all of America. All I can say is GOD BLESS AMERICA!!

LARRY THE ENGINEER AND VOMITUS COMITATUS

When I began driving, I always knew that eventually someone would throw up in or near my car. I never thought that person would be me.

A little background: I had been on a self-designed diet

that consisted of eating only a vegetable "stew" of my own creation.[42] I made enough "stew" for a week and reheated some to eat every night. One night, when the "stew" was almost a week old and I was in a hurry to pick up Larry and Sally, I ate the stuff cold. That was a bad idea.

Shortly thereafter, I picked up Larry and his wife, Sally, at the airport. Larry was an engineer from Minnesota. I had driven him before when we had discussed an interesting engineering dilemma arising from the 9/11 terrorist attack on New York City. Larry felt there was something fishy about the collapse of World Trade Center Building #7. He said the only buildings that should have collapsed were the two towers struck by the airliners. The steel frame of Building #7 was not physically compromised and should have easily withstood the ensuing fire. Larry wasn't a conspiracy theorist and he seemed to know what he was talking about. When I asked him if he thought aliens, white supremacists, or the Israelis had anything to do with the attack and subsequent collapse of WTC #7, Larry just smiled.

After I picked up Larry and Sally, we began a twenty-five-minute drive to their home. About fifteen minutes had passed, I began to feel dizzy and had to pull over to clear my head. I resumed driving, but a few minutes later, I had to stop again because I began to feel even dizzier. Larry offered to drive and I accepted.

After Larry had been driving for a few minutes, I felt even dizzier and began to feel nauseous. Larry and Sally suggested we go to Physician's Regional Hospital, which was only a

---

42   Lots of corn, some crushed tomatoes, some peas, and a little okra, all mixed with a can of chicken soup. (It's surprisingly good and very low in calories.)

few miles away. Somehow, even though the dizziness and nausea were getting worse, I agreed.

By the time we got to the Emergency Room, I was so dizzy, I couldn't stand and I was obliged to stumble/roll out of the car. Then, I began to violently vomit. The nurses brought out a wheelchair, to which I had to crawl, making sure my mouth wasn't aimed in my direction of travel.

Everything after that is a little hazy, but I remember offering Larry and Sally my car to get home. They said thanks but decided to call another Uber driver.

Back in the hospital, I was given an air sickness bag and hoisted onto an Emergency Room bed. I don't quite remember what happened next, but there was some poking, prodding, injecting, drawing blood, and sliding me into an MRI machine. I was tested for Covid (fortunately, negative) and for alcohol and drugs (unfortunately, also negative—I was a hippie, remember). Finally, after a few hours, when I began to feel somewhat normal and was ready to be discharged, the nurse told me I had had food poisoning. I knew exactly what food poisoned me. I learned an important lesson that night. I will never eat previously cooked unheated food again!

I called Larry the next day and told him the trip (and the entertainment) was on me. Both he and Sally seemed sincerely concerned about me, but they never called me for another trip! I don't really blame him.

THE FIFTH THIRD PRIVATE BANKER AND PROHIBITION

Naples has many banks, but the one with the strangest name is the Fifth Third Bank. I always wondered where the name came from. Could it be the bank's founders weren't sure whether their bank was the fifth or the third in whatever town they originated in? Or was the bank saying they were two-thirds better than any other bank (five-thirds equals one and two-thirds)?

My speculations were answered one night when I drove a member of Fifth Third Bank's Private Banking Division and his wife to a restaurant. We talked about the bank and he explained that the name came about in 1908, in Cincinnati, Ohio when The Third National Bank and The Fifth National Bank merged. They were going to call the merged bank the Third Fifth Bank, but prohibition was rearing its ugly head and the management thought Third Fifth sounded a lot like three-fifths, a measurement of liquor. So, they settled on the name Fifth Third Bank.

> **NOTES ON THE MEANING OF LIFE**—The gents at Fifth Third were right about the prohibition movement. On January 17, 1920, the United States banned the manufacturing, sale, transportation, importation, exportation, furnishing, or possession (*but not the drinking*) of any intoxicating liquor. Fortunately, the ban was ignored by most Americans and eventually repealed.

The Private Banker's knowledge of Private Banking impressed me even more than his knowledge of prohibition. As a lawyer, I had dealt with private bankers during my career, some of whom didn't know dividend from a pink sheet. Not so with my Fifth Third friend. He knew his stuff.

BLUE MARTINI LOUNGE, THE HOOSEGOW,

AND BACK AGAIN

One Year's Eve, I worked long hours and took a lot of passengers to and from a lot of bars and restaurants. On one trip, I drove a slightly disheveled twenties-something Bostonian to Blue Martini, a nice, upscale (i.e., expensive) bar/nightclub in the Mercato.

That night, the Mercato looked different than usual. There were scores of sheriff's deputies everywhere. Some were on foot, some were in cars, and a few were even on horses. The deputies were well groomed and well behaved and seemed more like chaperones at a dance than police officers searching for perps.

> **NOTES ON THE MEANING OF LIFE**—Score is an archaic measurement that means 20. Other interesting arcane, mostly old-fashioned measures are: furlong (1/8 of a mile), league (3 miles), cubit (18 inches), fathom (6 feet), fortnight (14 days), wee dram (an unquantified amount of alcohol for one drink), long ton (2,240 pounds), pennyweight (0.054857 ounces), rod (16 feet), nanocentury (one billionth of a century or 3.155 seconds), stone (14 pounds), stadium (607.14 feet), googol (1 followed by 100 zeroes or 10^{100}), googolplex (a googol to the power of a googol), smidgen (1/2 a pinch or 1/32 of a teaspoon), twain (2), hobbit (2 ½ bushels), and pottie (2 quarts).

I dropped off the passenger, wished him luck. I didn't expect to see him again, but I did!

The next morning (January 1) I started driving early. My

first call was to the Collier County jail. Just as I arrived, my twenties-something friend from Boston stumbled out of the building and wobbled toward Red Flame. He didn't look too good. When he got into my car, he looked even worse. He also exuded a strange (but not awful) combination of body odor, alcohol, institutional odor, and, for some reason, plastic.

"What happened?" I asked.

"I am not sure," he answered. "I drank a lot and got arrested. I think the policeman said I interfered with him."

"Did you?"

"I am not quite sure. I might have yelled at him, or pushed him, or threw up on him." Then he quickly added, "I feel like hell."

He looked worse than he felt. On the way home, I asked what he would be doing the rest of his stay in Naples.

"I'll probably go back to Blue Martini," he replied.

GATE GUARD VS. LAWYER—ROUND 1

One night, I drove a slightly intoxicated, relatively young passenger to his home in a gated community in the northern part of Naples. As we stopped at the guardhouse, the guard, who looked a lot like John Shaft (Richard Roundtree, not Samuel L. Jackson), asked for our licenses. Immediately the slightly drunk passenger began to complain to the guard. He added a few comments and mild epithets as he handed over his license. When the guard ignored the passenger, he notified the guard that he was a lawyer and he was going to sue the guard and the community for . . . well, he never said what. (Aren't some lawyers just pains in the ass?) I thought, but didn't tell him, that suing the community you live in and the guard who lets you in every day is probably not a good idea.

> **NOTES ON THE MEANING OF LIFE**—Richard Roundtree played John Shaft (he's the cat who won't cop out, when there's danger all about) in the 1971 film *Shaft*. Samuel L. Jackson played John Shaft II in the 2019 and 2020 films.

The guard took what seemed like forever (certainly intentionally) to examine the lawyer's license and then threw it back into the car, inadvertently hitting me in the ear, but, unlike the passenger, I didn't even think of suing!

"Do you want to see my license also?" I asked the guard, rather meekly.

"No, you're good."

THE OLD MAN AND THE SUPERMARKET

Every week or so, I was called to take an elderly passenger named Sam from his apartment off Pine Ridge to the nearby Publix Supermarket so he could buy his week's food. The trip was noticeably short, about a quarter mile, but Sam and I had a lot of interesting conversations, which made it worthwhile. One day, when I picked up Sam, he told me he wasn't going to Publix. Instead, he asked me to take him to Wynns Market, an upscale food emporium a little farther away. He was excited because, that week, he could buy posher food. I was excited because, that week, I would earn a posher fare.

MONEY TALKS! AND SOMETIMES, IT INHALES!

I drove many passengers to and from Port Royal, Naples' wealthiest neighborhood and, with one exception, they were all courteous, friendly, and down to earth

The one exception was an interesting case. He was courteous and friendly all right, but his feet didn't appear to be anywhere near the ground.

My adventure began when I arrived at a Port Royal driveway gate. I waited a while and, when no one showed up, I called the passenger.

"Hello, this is Al from Uber," I volunteered. "I am waiting in your driveway."

"Why are you waiting in my driveway?" he answered and asked.

"You called an Uber driver. I'm him."

"I did? You are?" was the passenger's retort.

By now, I could almost smell the cannabis wafting through the phone, but I (professionally) pressed on, "Yes, did you call an Uber driver?"

"I don't know."

Perhaps I should keep it simple, I thought, so I asked, "Do you want to go someplace?"

"Right now?"

To save time and bring our conversation (and my potential passenger's feet) back to Earth, I suggested, "Why don't you cancel this trip and when you're ready to go somewhere, call another Uber."

"Good idea," he replied, "Thanks."

As a precaution, I added, "Press cancel on your Uber app and then hang up the phone."

He did and Red Flame and I moseyed off to our next pickup.

THE SUPER-SIZED SERVICE ANIMAL

Uber requires all drivers to accept service animals, even if their dander causes a driver fatal anaphylactic shock. Uber's credo seems to be, "The animal must get through!" I drove many (mainly female) passengers who had cute little dogs, who may or may not have been service animals, without a second thought. However, one day I got called for a trip and immediately received the passenger's text asking, "We have a service animal. He's big! Any problem?"

I texted back, "What kind of animal is he and how big is he?"

"A German shepherd. Very big," was the response.

I grew up with animals and figured, what the hey. So, I texted back, "I'll be there."

When I arrived at the pickup, I saw two young fellows and a very large German shepherd waiting for me. The dog didn't faze me because he seemed friendly (he was) and he looked just like Smokey, my childhood pet.

The trip went smoothly and I dropped off men and beast at the Mercato. My human passengers seemed to be physically and mentally healthy, and, from the way they talked, were highly successful with women. As I was driving to my next pickup, I couldn't help wondering why either one of them needed a service animal.

FIRST YOU TAKE A DRINK, THEN THE DRINK TAKES YOU!

Although I usually didn't drive late at night, I have had my share of drunk (or otherwise sozzled—yes, it's a real word!) passengers. I am often asked by sober passengers what it is like to drive drunks (that's drive drunks, not drive drunk). Many assumed these passengers would be a problem, but they weren't. All the drunk (or otherwise sozzled) passengers I had driven fell into one of two categories: passed-out drunks, who were fine because my Uber driver app told me where to deposit them; and "funny" drunks, who insisted on telling jokes. None of the jokes the "funny" drunks told were, by themselves, very funny, but the way the drunks eventually told (or tried to tell) them was usually hilarious.

I picked up my first obviously drunk passenger on Fifth Avenue South in downtown Naples. When he got into the car, he tried to talk, but could only mumble something about a "scottle of botch". Then he appeared to fall asleep. Following the directions on my Uber driver app, we began our journey.

As we were driving north on Goodlette-Frank Road, passing the Bayfront housing/eating/drinking complex, my mute passenger quickly showed the world that he was still awake and could utter at least eight words of English. As I stopped at a traffic light, he quickly jumped up, bellowed, "Wait, there's a bar here—let me out," opened the door, and flung himself from the car. Luckily, we weren't moving, but I don't think he noticed. As he let the car, he stumbled and fell to the ground, but quickly got up, gave me a wave, and ran like a bat out of hell toward one of Bayfront's watering holes.

Later in my Uber career, I picked up a genuinely nice elderly couple at Fort Myers Beach. They had spent their day at the beach with their Buds, if you know what I mean. When I started taking them home, the gentleman (and he was a gentleman) politely asked me if he could have one last Budweiser on the way. Since I was a lawyer, a whole flood of legal issues quickly entered my mind: actual knowledge, intent, consent, respondeat superior, negligence, clean hands, and moral turpitude. This was my first "Can I drink beer in your Uber car?" request and I didn't know how to manage the situation. I didn't want to appear unfriendly. The passenger seemed like a nice guy, but I wasn't sure of what to do, so I punted. I told him drinking alcohol during a ride was against Uber's rules. I felt bad forcing him to stay thirsty, but he understood.

Of course, when I got home that night, I looked up the law so I would know what to do the next time a passenger wants to drink his Buds, rather than chat with them. It turns out Florida Statute §316.1936 prohibits *open* alcoholic beverages *that are immediately capable of being consumed* during the operation of a motor vehicle. The statute applies to drivers and passengers alike.

Well, I had made the right decision, but I thought the wording of this law a little strange. What if the occupant of a car has a can of Budweiser that is open but is not immediately capable of being consumed because it is too cold to drink (or is a brand he doesn't drink)? Would he be breaking the law?

That wasn't the only time alcohol or illegal drugs reared their head in Red Flame. On several occasions, I noticed a passenger furtively moving a paper bag to their mouths and sometimes I detected the odor of weed after a passenger left the car. (As a child of the '60s I know weed—we called it grass—when I smell it.)

Red Flame and I also experienced two other drug incidents of note. The first occurred as I arrived at a passenger's house. I looked in the rearview mirror and noticed he had just finished inhaling (i.e., snorting) what looked like a white powder. As soon as I stopped, the passenger quickly exited Red Flame and ran into his house. Merely out of curiosity, I quickly checked the entire back of the car but unfortunately the passenger didn't leave anything behind.

Another time a passenger told me he was going home to do coke (I'm pretty sure he meant caine, not-a-Cola) and asked me if I had a pusher. I wasn't sure if he meant drug dealer or drug implement,[43] but I told him I had neither.

TOM SAWYER GOIN' FISHIN'

Sometimes the space-time continuum loses its cohesion and an event that should be taking place in a different place and at a different time takes place in the here and now. Such an event occurred when I was called to the northern part of Naples to pick up a young man. When I arrived, I saw the spitting image of Tom Sawyer waiting for me. He was wearing a straw hat and what looked like hand-me-down clothes, and he was carrying two fishing poles. If he hadn't been wearing shoes, I'd have sworn I was back in antebellum St. Petersburg, Missouri.

---

43   A rod used to clear a screen from a coke pipe.

> **NOTES ON THE MEANING OF LIFE**—St. Petersburg, Missouri is the fictional setting of *Tom Sawyer* and *Huckleberry Finn*.

Even though "Tom" lived in one of the wealthiest communities around, he looked just like he was set to go fishin' in the crick.

After "Tom" got into the car, we said hello and he told me I was the third Uber driver he had called for this trip.

"What happened to the first two?" I queried.

"When they saw my fishing rods, they canceled."

I was a little surprised. The fishing rods weren't that long and looked brand new.

> **NOTES ON THE MEANING OF LIFE**—Many passengers wonder if, and why, an Uber driver can cancel a trip. We can, for any reason. The cancelation doesn't affect the driver's income, but if he cancels more than 4 percent of his trips, he forfeits some of the non-cash bonuses that Uber offers. I didn't understand "Tom's" cancelations. Transporting two brand-new six-foot fishing rods and a polite young man isn't that heavy a lift!

I dropped "Tom" off at a little stream near Estey Avenue aptly called Rock Creek (aka Rock Crick). After he got out of the car, I looked, but neither Huck nor Jim had arrived yet!

NORTH TO ALASKA

'Twas the day before Christmas and all through the streets, drove Alan from Uber, seeking riders to meet.[44]

Christmas Eve is an interesting and fun day to drive for Uber. The passengers are friendlier, they are on time, and they offer the most interesting stories.

The first ride on my first Christmas Eve was to the airport. I picked up a rider who, as you will see, was ironically named Sam. After we began talking, he said he was going to his sister's house for Christmas.

"Where does your sister live?" I asked.

"In Alaska, a little southeast of Nome."

"Don't you two have things a little backwards?" I again inquired. "Shouldn't your sister be coming here to spend Christmas in Florida with you? After all, Florida is a lot warmer than Alaska, ESPECIALLY IN LATE DECEMBER!"

"I know, but she wanted me to come there" was his response.

As our conversation continued, I asked if there was a lot of snow in Nome.

"Well," he replied, "not much until last weekend when they got six feet."

A paraphrase of Dorothy Gale came to mind and I exclaimed, "There's no place like Nome!"

NOTES ON THE MEANING OF LIFE—At the end of the 1939 film _The Wizard of Oz_, Dorothy is finally transported

44   Apologies to Clement Clark Moore

> home when she clicks her ruby slippered heels together
> and repeats, "There's no place like home."

Sam and I kept talking. He said his trip would take over twelve hours. Hmm, this meant he would be in the skies of Alaska close to midnight! Initially, I was worried, but then I remembered that Santa's sled has anti-collision lights!

When we arrived at the airport, Sam said goodbye and got out of the car. I wished him Godspeed on his trip to his sister's house, below that old white mountain, just a little southeast of Nome.

> **NOTES ON THE MEANING OF LIFE**—The theme song from the classic 1960 Western (well, Northern), *North to Alaska*, tells of how prospector Sam McCord (played by John Wayne—"a mighty man in the year of nineteen-one")[45] discovers gold below that old white mountain, just a little southeast of Nome.

THERE AND BACK AGAIN. AND THERE AGAIN!

The time: later that Christmas Eve

The scene: A heavily wooded apartment complex in northern Naples on Christmas Eve. A young couple, Nadia and Art, are toting their luggage to a waiting Uber car where the helpful Uber driver is helping them put the bags into the

---

45 *North to Alaska*, written by Johnny Horton and Tillman Franks

trunk. The couple is going to the airport so they can fly to Ohio and spend Christmas with their family. Like many Americans, they are going home for the holidays.

> **NOTES ON THE MEANING OF LIFE**—The phrase "Home for the holidays" originated in the early nineteenth century when pioneers, mostly from Massachusetts, upstate New York, and Connecticut, settled in the Northwest Territory (modern-day Indiana, Illinois, and Ohio). Since it took almost three weeks for these settlers to travel back east, the tradition developed of traveling home only once a year, at Christmas. This annual trek became known as "going home for the holidays."

The crisis: As the Uber car approaches the airport, Nadia realizes that she forgot her I.D. at home! The driver stops the car in a nearby parking lot where Nadia, Art, and the Uber driver rifle through the couple's luggage, searching for Nadia's I.D. No luck. Fortunately, Nadia remembers that she left her I.D. on the kitchen table. The flight leaves in an hour and a half and the apartment is twenty-six miles away! What can be done?

The resolution: The Uber driver, experienced in crisis management, takes charge, and orders—er, suggests—that the couple get back into the car so all can "fly" back to the apartment, pick up the missing I.D., and return to the airport in time for the flight.

The driver puts Red Flame into sport mode, engages hyperdrive (Editor's Note: there is no such thing as hyperdrive in an Audi), and zooms back to the couple's apartment, carefully following auto racer Dan Gurney's sage advice never to exceed 175 miles per hour (Editor's Note: No one went near 175 miles per hour.) and blasting Ozzie and Black Sabbath singing/bellowing *Paranoia* so all would stay in the right mood.

> **NOTES ON THE MEANING OF LIFE**—The Cannonball Baker Sea-to-Shining-Sea Memorial Trophy Dash is an auto race from the Red Ball Garage on 8th Avenue in Manhattan to the Portofino Inn in Redondo Beach, California. It has been run intermittently since 1972 and has only one rule: you must stay on the ground! After Dan Gurney and Brock Yates won the inaugural race with a time of 35 hours, 54 minutes (current record: 25 hours, 39 minutes), Gurney famously stated, "And we never exceeded 175 miles per hour."

Conclusion the first: The trio arrives at the apartment, Nadia retrieves her I.D., and the group "flies" back to the airport, arriving just in the (Saint) Nick of time. Nadia and Art make their flight. Nadia, Art, and the Uber driver all conclude that their mutual success was a gift from baby Jesus on the eve of his birthday. (Editor's Note: We'll give him this one; after all, it's Christmas.)

The Grinch/Scrooge rears his ugly head: Even though the Uber driver (Yes, it was me!) drove over seventy-eight miles and for more than two hours to make sure Art and Nadia had a merry Christmas, Uber Technologies, Inc. only paid him for a one-way trip from Nadia's and Art's apartment to the airport. When repeatedly asked for the correct fare, Uber Technologies would only tell the driver, "You were paid the correct fare."[46]

Conclusion the second: In the spirit of Christmas, the Uber driver forgives the ungodly parsimonious weasels at Uber Technologies, Inc. and is happy he helped a young couple get home to their families for the holidays. He also appreciates the couple's generous Christmas tip!

THE RUSSKIES, SECRET POLICE, AND INTERNATIONAL CONFLICT ON LIVINGSTON ROAD

While Naples is the home to people of almost every ethnicity, only a few Russians live here. In fact, I only drove Russians twice. Both rides were very interesting!

Early in my Uber career, I picked up a young Russian couple and drove them to a public (aka people's) park near the zoo. During the drive, they explained that in Russia, the government controls everything, including Uber (Yandex in Russia) drivers. Then they very innocently asked me if I had to provide the police with the names and destinations of all my passengers.

Well, I replied, "Only those who don't leave an adequate tip!"

Fortunately, they laughed.

The next time I drove Russians, I drove a couple in their

---

46   I called Uber five times to try to collect the correct fare. Each time they promised that they would send an e-mail and resolve the problem in forty-eight hours. Never got an e-mail and the problem was never resolved. After spending over four hours with them on the phone, I gave up!

early forties. The trip occurred shortly after Russia invaded Ukraine. As my passengers and I were driving down Livingston Road, we ran smack dab into one of my old favorites, an anti-war protest. There were scores of demonstrators on both sides of the road, waving Ukrainian flags and chanting, both in English and a foreign language that I supposed was Ukrainian, what I assumed were dreadful things about Russians.

The male passenger went ballistic. He began screaming at the demonstrators, even though the windows were closed. I didn't know exactly what he was saying, but he repeatedly used the word *mat* (which means mother in Russian) and hissed a lot.

I thought of humming a few bars of the State Anthem of The Soviet Union to ramp up the excitement, but quickly thought better of it and just drove the Godless commies to their destination.

THE TINY, YOUNG, PREGNANT, HISPANIC MOM AND REDEMPTION!

Besides being fun, driving for Uber also builds (or, in my case, restores) character. I had the opportunity to drive a passenger from the Walmart Neighborhood Market in the Carillon Place shopping mall to her apartment. God gave me this this opportunity four times and I needed all four to improve myself as a person and to show compassion toward my fellow man (in this case, toward a very tiny, very young, very pregnant, and very Hispanic fellow woman).

The first time I was called to pick up this woman, she was waiting outside the supermarket, standing next to two shopping carts that were overflowing with groceries. When I got out of the car, she just looked at me, said, "No hablo ingles," and got into the back seat of Red Flame.

Then I realized I was supposed to load all the groceries by myself. I immediately felt put upon, but I loaded the groceries and drove to the woman's apartment, which was about 2,600 feet (i.e., a half-mile) away. When we arrived, the woman got out of her car, walked to her door, and again, just waited.

Good God, I thought, *I am going to have to unload the groceries as well*. Now I really felt put upon, but I unloaded them anyway.

The woman didn't say a word. She just unlocked her door and went inside. As I was driving away, I noticed I had earned a fare of $2.20, and the passenger didn't leave a tip. Curses, put upon a third time!

A few weeks later the same scenario was repeated. Again, I loaded two shopping carts of groceries, drove 2,600 feet, unloaded the groceries, earned a fare of $2.20, and got no tip. This time I felt worse than put upon, I felt like a speed bag.

> **NOTES ON THE MEANING OF LIFE**—A speed bag is a small punching bag used by boxers for practicing quick punches.

The next week, I was again called to Walmart and saw the same woman (again with two full shopping carts) waiting for me. *Damn*, I thought, *I am not going to take it anymore*. So, I stopped the car, opened the trunk, got back into the car, and pretended to read something until the woman finished putting the groceries in the trunk. When we got to her apartment, I, once again, popped open the trunk, pretended to read, and waited for the woman to unload all the groceries from my trunk. Then I drove away.

Yea, I thought, *I "won."* But I didn't feel too good about it. Of course, I quickly realized that I didn't win. In fact, I lost my humanity. I had just "forced" a very pregnant, very tiny woman to load and then unload fifteen somewhat heavy bags of groceries. At minimum, my behavior was crude and rude; at worst, it was f***ed up. I even violated my long-held Flower Child and Cowboy ideals of fairness, decency, and compassion towards my fellow man (and woman).

Fortunately, I got a chance at redemption. A week later, I was called to Walmart a fourth time, by the same woman, with the same loaded shopping carts. But this time, things were different because I acted differently. As I stopped the car, I popped the trunk, jumped out, opened the back door, and motioned the woman to sit down. After she got in the car, I closed her door, loaded the groceries into the trunk, closed the trunk, and wheeled the empty cart to a nearby Walmart employee who was on cart collection duty. Then, I quickly (but safely) drove the usual 2,600 feet to the woman's apartment.

When we arrived, I again popped the trunk, jumped out, ran around to the woman's door, opened it for her (and closed it behind her), and then carried all the groceries to the front door of the woman's apartment.

As I was driving away, I again noticed the woman didn't leave a tip, but this time I didn't care. In fact, I'm glad she didn't. I felt like a better person as I had ultimately shown fairness, decency, and compassion to my fellow man (in this case, my fellow woman). My long-lost Hippie ideals and cowboy credentials had returned. Thank you, God for giving me a fourth chance!

CHAPTER 6

A Death in the Family

My many years of rugged and exciting adventures riding the trail with Red Flame ended abruptly on a bright, summer day as we were moseying down I-75.

Like most elderly steeds, Red Flame was showing his age. He had been suffering from Timing Belt Toxoplasmosis for some time and had received a timing belt transplant at an urgent care facility earlier in the year. Unfortunately, the operation wasn't a complete success: he still had a nagging cough and occasionally experienced the shakes. But being the tough German that he was, Red Flame kept both his spirits and acceleration up until the very end.

That end came as we were driving three young girls to the airport. As we were purring along at 75 mph, Red Flame breathed his last. He suffered a massive Cardiac Timing Belt Infarction that caused his pistons to smash his valves and his camshafts to splinter. He was dead before he rolled to a stop.

I was distraught and felt helpless. Fortunately, the girls in the car were neither distraught nor helpless. Far from it. They told me not to worry and sprang into action. They called another Uber, who quickly arrived, made sure I was safe, and whisked the girls to their awaiting flight. Red Flame and I were left on the side of the road.

Red Flame was eventually taken by ambulance (i.e., tow truck) to the morgue (i.e., repair shop), where doctors (i.e., mechanics) declared him deader than a doornail. His remains were interred in a local potter's field (i.e., junkyard).

NOTES ON THE MEANING OF LIFE—A potter's field is a place for the burial of unknown, unclaimed, or indigent people and cars. (Editor's Note: No, not cars.)

Even though I was in mourning for Red Flame, I was able to rustle up a relatively new Teutonic mount, a black BMW. I dubbed him Black Bandit and we bonded almost instantly. The Bandit more than adequately filled Red Flame's tires. He had newer electronics and a brighter (sandalwood) interior than Red Flame's deep black cabin. From the first time we met, I knew we would get along. Although Red Flame will always have a special place in my heart, I enjoy my time with The Bandit, still riding the trail alone, collecting and dispensing passengers along the way.

CHAPTER 7

All Good Things . . .

In the immortal words of my old (very old) friend, Geoffrey Chaucer, all good things must come to an end. My yearlong romance with Uber ended on a warm night outside the Dollar Tree store in the Carillon Place shopping center. As I arrived to pick up the passenger (this was my other bad passenger), I saw that she was not alone. Her mother and three siblings, including a newborn, were all in tow. The passenger, a woman in her twenties, quickly opened the door and immediately upbraided me for not wearing my mask. (It was hooked on my ear, so I quickly put it on.) Everyone then piled into the car. The elderly mother got into the front, and the passenger and her three siblings, including the car-seated newborn, got in the back.

As soon as the ride began, the two preteen male siblings began to fistfight. As they were flailing around and screaming, one of them whacked me in the back of the head. I politely asked them to calm down. They didn't and, in less than a minute, I got whacked in the head a second time.

Strangely, as we neared our destination, the young woman passenger asked me to stop and let everyone out before we reached their building in the apartment complex. I did what she asked.

After they had left the car, I looked in the back and saw both front seatbacks had been torn off and were lying on the floor.

I got out of the car and called to my rapidly departing passengers that they had broken both seatbacks. Although none of the family seemed to understand much English during the ride, they suddenly remembered at least three English words and, while retreating, shouted, "F*** you, f*** you, f*** you, a**hole."

After I had gathered myself together, I realized why they wanted to be let out before their destination. It was so I wouldn't see their exact address.

To make a short story even shorter, Red Flame suffered $410 in damage and I missed a day of work getting estimates for repair. I presumed Uber would either reimburse me or would provide me with the passenger's name and address so I could make a claim for the damage they caused.

Boy was I wrong. Even after sending Uber photographs of the damage and a written estimate of repair, they told me they would only give me a $250 "inconvenience fee" (which, they said, was the maximum "allowed"). They wouldn't give me the passenger's name or address because, they said, they respected a passenger's privacy above all else. Apparently, "all else" includes a driver's personal safety and the safety of his property.

I didn't know where else to turn. I dithered back and forth on the subject for weeks until I found inspiration in the words of another famous author who faced a similar problem.

NOTES ON THE MEANING OF LIFE

To be, or not to be, that is the question:

Whether 'tis nobler in the mind to suffer

The slings and arrows of outrageously destroyed seatbacks,

Or to take arms in Small Claims Court

And by opposing, collect $410 in damages.

–Apologies to W. Shakespeare and Hamlet,
late Prince of Denmark

In the end, I didn't go to court, but I did fire off a letter of complaint to the president of Uber Technologies, Inc. I tried to make the letter lighthearted, yet meaningful. I don't think I succeeded. In the letter, I introduce myself to the president of Uber Technologies, Inc. as a lowly Uber driver from Naples, Florida. I describe the damage done to my car and to me by my criminally destructive passengers. I also describe their abusive language directed at me. I then ask Uber's President why Uber was protecting passengers who were criminals (and vandalistic) and screwing one of his lowly Uber drivers.

Unsurprisingly, Uber never responded to my letter.

While I admired Uber's passenger privacy policy (as all Uber passengers should), I couldn't believe they would protect a criminal (vandalism and assault are crimes) to the detriment of a driver. After Uber's policy and actions sunk in, my warm and fuzzy feeling for them was gone. I still like driving for them, but I no longer think of them as a family. I now just consider them a mere company providing a service.

On a humorous note, I recognize that if a passenger ever castrates an Uber driver, Uber will protect the passenger with their dying breath, but will only provide the driver a $250 "inconvenience fee." Well, at least the fee's name is appropriate. After all, most men would consider castration, at minimum, an inconvenience.

CHAPTER 8

Denouement

> **NOTES ON THE MEANING OF LIFE**—Denouement means "the final part of a narrative in which the strands of the plot are drawn together and explained or resolved."

I still drive for Uber. Partially because they still whisk anyone to their destination in a private automobile driven by a friendly and efficient Uber driver at a reasonable fare.[47] But mainly because I get to drive interesting passengers who tell interesting stories. And I consider myself a veteran Uber driver because I have been driving long enough to hear repeats of the same stories.

I now also consider myself a veteran Neapolitan because I have been here long enough to have known aspects of Naples that are now long gone.

The first restaurant that caught my eye right after I moved to Naples was St. George and the Dragon on Fifth Avenue South. I liked its cool name. Passengers told me the waiters and waitresses wore tuxedos. They also said that "George's" onion rings were the best in town. I looked forward to eating

---

47   Although they are rapidly increasing.

Former Site of St. George and the Dragon

there, but before I had a chance, the restaurant closed and was slowly dismantled.

Likewise, I always wanted to see the dog races at the Naples-Fort Myers Greyhound Track in Bonita Springs, but before I knew it, they were gone too. Hopefully, the swamp buggy racetrack off Collier Boulevard will stay open for a while because watching a swamp buggy race is the last item on my bucket list.

I finally know how my passengers felt when their favorite bar, restaurant, road, or even nudist colony vanished and now exists only as a happy memory.

As I finish my story, all I can say is, "Ahh, it's a shame things had to change."

Well, that's it! I hope you enjoyed the book. Thanks for your time!!

THE CONCLUSION OF THE MEANING OF LIFE—I finally made it to Easy Street! (Although, curiously, it is in Port Charlotte, not Naples.)

And I lived happily ever after!

Finis

"After all, it's what we've done that makes us what we are."

~J. Croce

The Naples Almanac

Almanac A - Map of The City of Naples

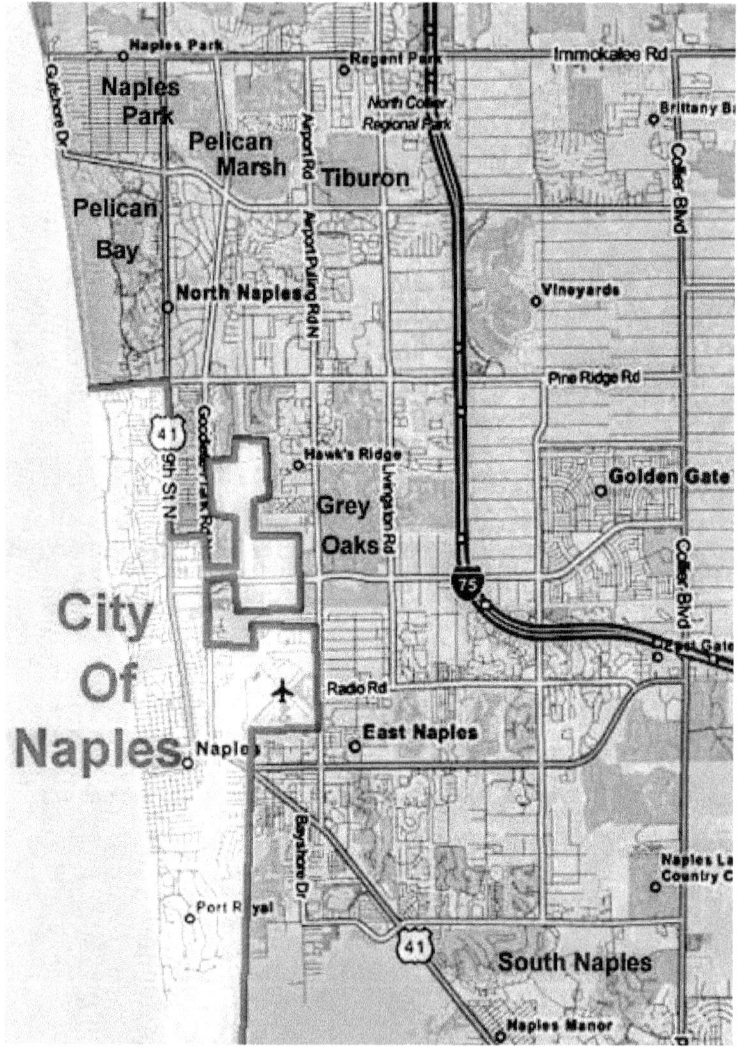

Almanac B – Map of Collier County Showing County Regions

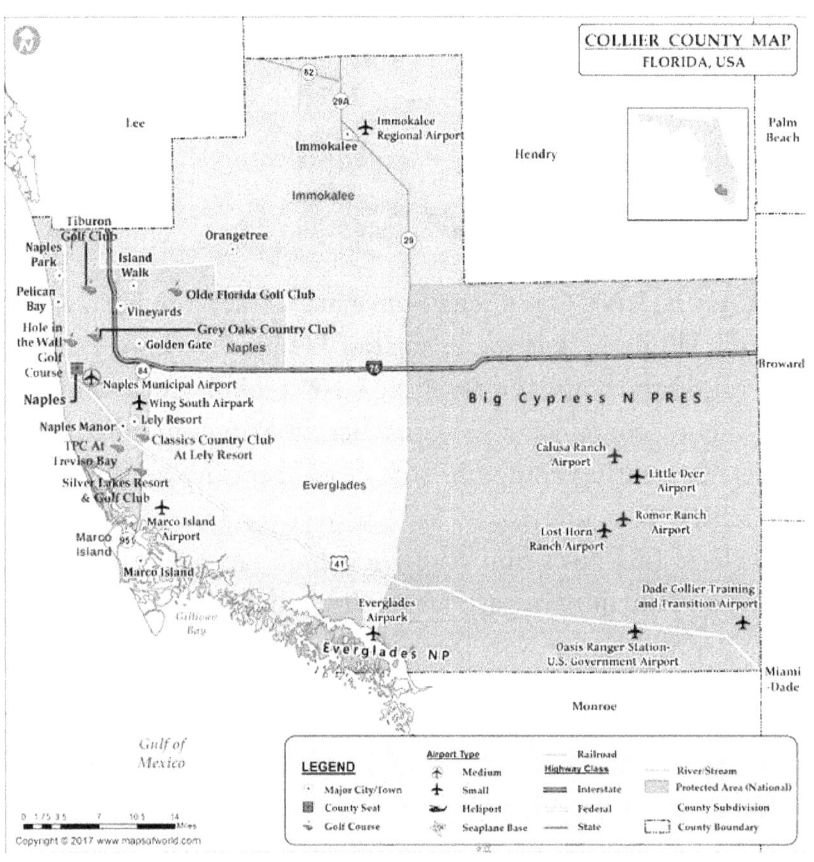

Populated Area of Naples

About the Author

ALAN BIANCO is a renaissance man, at least in his own mind. While he has spent most of his life as a lawyer, he has also been employed repairing street potholes, delivering cosmetics, announcing polo matches, stocking supermarket shelves, creating computer software, operating a website, teaching at a university, and inspecting apartments in Harlem. This gives him a unique (some say skewed) outlook on humanity in particular and life in general.

Al grew up in New York (although he was born in Newark, NJ). Like many of his elderly New York countrymen, he moved to Florida to get a tan and pay less taxes. Now a resident of Naples, he enjoys all aspects of Neapolitan life, except driving behind a Flying Florida Pick (see page 76) or waiting at the slowest traffic lights in the Western Hemisphere.

Naples Secrets in the Sun is Al's first attempt at creative writing, but not his first attempt at humor (that would be his political humor website: meaningoflifesatire.com).